AGRIBUSINESS PROJECT APPRAISAL
Theory and Applications

J. P. Hella and D. W. Ndyetabula

Adonis & Abbey Publishers Ltd
St James House
13 Kensington Square,
London, W8 5HD
United Kingdom

Website: http://www.adonis-abbey.com
E-mail Address: editor@adonis-abbey.com

Nigeria:
Suites C4 & C5 J-Plus Plaza
Asokoro, Abuja, Nigeria
Tel: +234 (0) 7058078841/08052035034

British Library Cataloguing-in-Publication Data
A catalogue record for this book is available from the British Library

ISBN: 978-1-909112-68-1

AGRIBUSINESS PROJECT APPRAISAL
Theory and Applications

J. P. Hella and D. W. Ndyetabula

ADONIS & ABBEY
PUBLISHERS LTD

Table of Contents

CHAPTER EIGHT
Agribusiness Project Monitoring, Evaluation and Impact Assessment .191

List of Tables

List of Figures

List of Boxes

List of Appendices

Foreword

In developing countries like Tanzania, planning, implementation and evaluation of agricultural projects can be a daunting task. To be able to overcome the challenges, one needs to use a comprehensive methodology for project formulation, planning, execution, monitoring and evaluation. Unfortunately, not many coherent and straightforward methodologies for project management exist in developing countries. Books that prescribe straight forward procedures for project initiation, planning, execution and closing in a developing country context are practically non-existent. This book is therefore timely as it does prescribe effective and successful initiation and execution of projects in agribusiness.

With its specific context of a developing country, this book explains the entire project life cycle in details, focusing on analytical and appraisal techniques. Project management professionals and students will find this book useful as it efficiently explains the process of project formulation and execution.

Senkondo, E. M. M
Professor of Agricultural Economics
Department of Food and Resource Economics
School of Agricultural Economics and Business Studies
Sokoine University of Agriculture

Preface

This book is about Agribusiness Project Appraisal. It applies fundamental and contemporary analytical methods necessary for formulating, planning, managing, analyzing, implementing, and monitoring a project. Though the methods are universal and can be applied in any situation, the perspective of this book is that of developing, transitional, and emerging economies within an agribusiness context. Our decision to write this book stems from a perceived need for project appraisal text in a specific agribusiness field.

In Agribusiness, a project is viewed as an investment activity in which *financial resources* are *expected* to create capital assets that produce benefits over an extended period. Two keywords are identified in this definition "expected" and "financial resources." The word *"expected,"* as it appears in the definition, has elements of uncertainty. *"Financial resources"* on the other hand, calls for proper planning and management. The two keywords combined develops the need to formulate, manage and evaluate projects.

You may all be familiar with the phrase "Fools rush in where angels fear to tread." An action of investing financial resources in an agribusiness project today has a specific future consequence. The consequences can be known, but with uncertainties. The action taken to ascertain the consequence is an initiative whose unique challenge is to determine whether the decision to invest financial resources in a certain project will be successful or foolish. Contemporary agribusiness project analytical methods presented in this book will provide guidance to readers on the determination of successful agribusiness project formulation.

This book is written to satisfy the needs of a wide audience including:

- Practitioners in the field of Agricultural Economics and project implementers,
- Instructors in project planning and management,
- Undergraduate and Postgraduate students majoring in Project Planning

The book is organized into eight chapters and one appendix. Chapter 1 provides an overview of the important concepts in project planning, analysis of projects, its relevance and purpose, and how it is understood from different perspectives. In subsequent chapters, the various steps involved in carrying out project management in particular project identification, are presented.

Chapter 2 gives an explanation of project management, the project cycle, or the stages through which a project passes. This helps in understanding the relevance of economic analysis at each stage and provides a backdrop against which project analysis may be viewed. Chapter 3 briefly describes the project identification through a participatory approach using traditional log-frame.

Chapter 4 deals with the method of identifying and quantifying the economic costs and benefits of a project. The chapter starts with identification of different costs and benefits in agribusiness projects and, thereafter, explains various adjustments that are required to arrive at the economic costs and benefits of a project. Chapter 5 presents techniques of agribusiness project analyses focusing on discounted and non-discounted measures of project worth such as payback period (PBP), Net Present Value (NPV), Benefit Cost Ratio and Internal Rate of Return (IRR).

Chapter 6 presents the methods of determining sensitivity analysis of agribusiness project appraisal while Chapter 7 deals with the implementation of agribusiness project activities. Chapter 8 deals with agribusiness project monitoring and evaluation as an important management tool necessary to help improve the efficiency of on-going projects and the selection and design of future projects.

The state of the art of this book is revealed by its progression, modest and outstanding arrangement that gives the reader a point of departure when thinking of formulating new and independent agribusiness project. We are adamant that the reader will find this text resourceful and suitable for theoretical and practical applications.

J. P. Hella   **D.W. Ndyetabula**

CHAPTER ONE

Project Planning: Important Concepts

1.1 Introduction

The agricultural sector in Tanzania has gone through several reforms including the famous Ujamaa (1967-1985) and the more recent liberalization phases from 1985 to date. Corta & Price (2009) identify the following problem-solution models for agricultural development in Tanzania:

a) *Problem*: Over-regulation of crop markets, monopoly power concentrated in larger cooperatives/private firms, corruption, low farm gate prices relative to export prices, lack of incentives to produce for cash.

   Solution: Lift regulations, reduce cooperative power, liberalize markets to raise farm gate prices and incentives to produce, do away with corruption.

b) *Problem*: Further liberalization will only enable traders to exploit farmers and keep farm gate prices low; resource poor farmers cannot afford inputs.

   Solution: Re-agrarianise Tanzania through pro-poor farming support via extension, selective input support (smart subsidies), credit, more secure markets/equitable inclusion in value chains, social protection to prevent asset stripping in crisis, enforcement of the minimum wages, secure women's land rights.

c) *Problem*: Green revolution in Africa has not worked so far and will not work in the future.

   Solution: Labour mobility to urban areas – remittances to rural areas. Just forget about agriculture, it will not work anyway.

In August 2009, the former president of Tanzania Dr. Jakaya Kikwete launched the initiative *Kilimo Kwanza* (Agriculture First) which addresses all the problems listed above. *Kilimo Kwanza* was initiated by the private sector through Tanzania National Business Council (TNBC) aimed at achieving a Green Revolution in Agriculture (United Republic of Tanzania, 2009). According to President Kikwete (2009), *Kilimo Kwanza* is a national resolve to accelerate agricultural transformation. It comprises a holistic set of policy instruments and strategic interventions towards addressing the various sectoral challenges and taking advantage of numerous opportunities to modernize and commercialize agriculture in Tanzania. The Tanzania Business Council (2009) put emphasis on the potential of agriculture in contributing towards national wealth creation and meeting global conditions for ensuring food and nutritional security.

Kilimo Kwanza focuses on modernization of agriculture, including both small and large scale farms, through technological and political reforms, public-private partnership, value chain approaches and foreign investments (TNBC, 2009). The difference that *Kilimo Kwanza* is expected to make is to mobilize the whole society, in particular the private sector, for a joint effort to boost agriculture by giving it priority and by pointing out the importance of agriculture for the county's future development. As young people are running away from agriculture and poverty is increasing among smallholder farmers and pastoralists, there is a need to change the perception that there is no future in agriculture in Tanzania and increase the sector's self-confidence and status.

Currently, the Agricultural Sector Development Programme (ASDP) is the main mechanism for support to agricultural development in the country and will probably be the implementing mechanism of *Kilimo Kwanza*. How do you invest in agriculture in a conducive way for boosting production, securing food security, creating job opportunities, improving smallholder farmers' livelihoods and taking care of the rights of local people?. Knowledge of agribusiness project planning and implementation is necessary.

This book attempts to provide a simple step-by-step approach for the agribusiness project planning and evaluation. This subject has been an active field of study and research since early 1960s and many articles, text books, and compendia have been written on it. However, many of these references are written in technical language which can be understood only by economists who have a good knowledge of mathematics.

Agribusiness development projects aim to change a present situation to an improved situation over time. A project is an instrument of change. Change processes have some basic common features. These include:

- The broader context in which a project is situated;
- A (problem) situation which must be changed;
- Objectives, or visions of the improved future situation, that should be achieved; and
- Choices about where and how to intervene through time with investments, actions and activities to achieve the envisaged improved future situation.

A project therefore represents a particular set of choices (or interventions) over time to move from a present situation to an envisaged future situation. The concept of development is dynamic and essentially a human phenomenon, i.e. what we (the target group) want and how it is to be achieved over time.

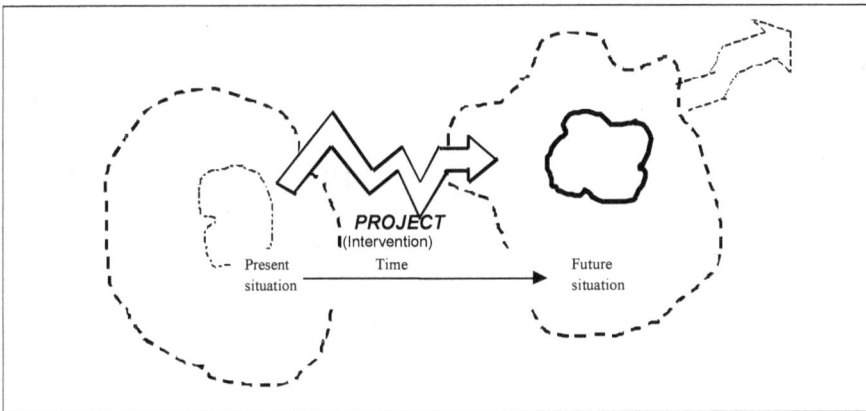

Figure 1.1: The Project Concept

1.2   Agribusiness Development Projects

Agribusiness development requires, among other things, an increase in profitability, productive job opportunities and greater achievement in the food and agricultural business sector. These should be accomplished with minimum, if any, damage, to the environment.

Agribusiness development projects such as those dealing with crop and livestock production, harnessing natural resources (water, land, etc.), those promoting technological innovation, improved production processes, improved human capacity, social welfare, etc. potentially offer an important methods to achieve development objectives.

When defining development projects, it is important first to distinguish between privately financed projects and projects that form part of government initiatives. Commercial agriculture project development is largely financed privately (e.g. a private farming operation). Within the framework of agribusiness development projects, the focus is largely on the flow of government funds and the possible mobilisation of the same. Such flow of funds is therefore often regarded as the central element in many definitions of projects. The FAO, for example, defines project planning as *"a proposal for investment where a cost stream results in a certain flow of benefits over a specified period"*.

World Bank publications expand on this idea and link project development to a flow of benefits. "Generally, in agricultural projects we are thinking of an investment asset from which we can expect to realize benefits over an extended period of time" (Gittinger, 1982). A project can also be viewed as a "proposal for capital investment to create opportunities for producing goods and services."

The criticism against the above definitions is that they mostly emphasize the technical aspect, i.e. capital input or financial flows, which leads directly to the creation of material assets, while no direct reference is made to the development functions of a project which include human development, distributional and social impacts. The contemporary view is that agribusiness development projects are primarily people-oriented and that provision must be made for the dynamic elements of change over time. Recent convention thus defined agribusiness project as follows:

A project is an instrument of change. It is a co-ordinated series of actions resulting from a decision to change resource combinations and levels so as to contribute to the realization of the country's development objectives.

Such a definition focuses on a project within broader development strategies, macro-economic objectives and policy of a country. Within this defined framework it is clear that agribusiness projects do not necessarily have to focus on production. Objectives such as job creation, capital formation (savings in foreign exchange), the uplifting of a target population, improvement of welfare for impoverished groups, the elimination of rural poverty, the redistribution of income, etc. should be strived for within development planning via the agribusiness project approach.

The question begging for answer now is *where does the project participants and, more precisely, the beneficiaries (farmers, etc.) fit into this definition?* One of the basic principles of economic project appraisal is that unless the individual participants benefit consistently more in the "with -project" in comparison with the "without project" scenario, projects will fail – target groups will not participate as there are no incentives in such activities.

Government also does have an important role to play to sustained beneficial status, through support in the technology development system, extension, rural infrastructure investment, etc. Such support could thus be considered, especially during start up phases of projects. Government should ensure that all supports are aligned with the policy objectives. However, if the long term economic and financial benefits do not exceed the costs, subsidization, social engineering and aligned policies will not guarantee sustainability and participation.

The definition of an agribusiness project should therefore be expanded to include the notions of interventions, participation and sustainability for all stakeholders and participants (including the farmers, businesses, financial transactions and also the public and private sector investors).This broader approach to defining a project allows project objectives to include aspects such as increased farm income, employment creation, distributional aspects including gender and youth, environmental aspects and national income and other economic growth dimensions. A wide range of criteria measuring micro, as well as macro impacts, will therefore be required to determine whether a project investment is justified or not.

These views also provide for an analytical framework for managing and analyzing information across the expected life of a project. It allows for comparison of several projects, or alternative designs of the same project. A major limitation/challenge of the project format, however, is its reliance on quality data estimates or projections of expected benefits and costs.

21

1.3 Classification of Agribusiness Development Projects

In the abovementioned views, the main emphasis is on change, participation and interventions as components of development. Many projects aimed at change in agriculture can therefore be seen in relation to development. The following seven functional classifications are useful:

1.3.1 Projects aimed at technological innovation

The objectives of these types of projects relate to the technical transformation of the agricultural sector. The issue here is the enhancement of technical effectiveness, while the goal is an increase in profit through an increase in physical production per unit, i.e. improved productivity.

The key to success of this type of project lies in offsetting of risks and uncertainty by participating farmers. Should there be a small degree of risk acceptance by participants and/or should technological innovation be extremely risky, a technology innovation of project cannot be given a fair chance of success, i.e. the *"with new technology"* situation may not be more beneficial as the *"without new technology"* situation.

1.3.2 Expanding the natural resource base

This type of project is aimed at change and development by unlocking natural resources such as water and land for production purposes. These projects are often tackled on a large scale and are often viewed as *"glamour projects"*. This type of project can make a tremendous contribution towards production and agricultural development. In rural development planning, however, it must also be viewed critically, *inter alia* because of the history of limited broad base impact of such projects on the general improvement in rural living standards. The group who benefits from this type of development is often small, while a large number of complementary inputs are required for the project to succeed. A greater impact is often observed where attention is instead paid to a number of smaller projects within a well-constructed development programme, i.e. constructing wells to sustain small-scale irrigation development and improving market facilities. This type of agricultural project should, only in exceptional cases, be incorporated into a rural strategy. The large-scale project approach is examined in more detail later.

1.3.3 Improving the living conditions of disadvantaged groups

This type of project aims to improve the general living conditions of specific groups. Here the issue is not to unlock natural resources per se. It can be seen instead as a "conscious public decision to intervene in the market process and change the ownership structure of the factors of production and to channel the projects' benefits towards designated target groups."

Projects in agricultural credit, rural settlement, land reform, food production and integrated rural development focusing on designated target group(s) are included in this category. Such projects clearly fall within the field of public sector assistance and participation rather than on the establishment of commercial agricultural production through optimal resource utilization.

1.3.4 Improved market infrastructure

Limited market infrastructure is hampering agricultural development in many rural settings. Improvement in market infrastructure is extremely important in developing market based agriculture. Harvesting, grading, storage and transportation may lead to a considerable increase in surplus food and fiber. However, such projects are not merely intended to support commercial programmes. Low-input, broad-focused programmes could also be supplemented by projects that stimulate the flow of inputs and proceeds.

1.3.5 Institutional capacity development

Modern agriculture requires a support system consisting of a number of functional components. These components are provided within an institutional framework. Institutional capacity is currently viewed as one of the most limiting factors in the process of agricultural and rural development. This type of institutionally oriented project aims, in particular, to create a human and organizational infrastructure that strengthens and supports local initiatives so that decision-making, the choice and implementation of programmes and projects, resource allocation and monitoring can take place on a more decentralized and informed basis.

Within these types of projects, the focus is on three levels: macro or central level, regional level and on the level of participating groups and individuals. The main objective is to improve effective participation. From this point of view, production may be constrained in the short term because more attention is given to human capacity development and mobilization, i.e. empowerment. In the long term, however, the development of capacity on each level may, to a large extent, give rise to increased production and productivity.

1.3.6 Multifunctional investment projects

A sixth type of project may be added, where more than one of the abovementioned functions is undertaken jointly within one project. With a commercialization approach it is in any case important that all inputs of the *"package"* are complementary to and reinforcing one another. An agribusiness project format as defined in section 1.1 provide a suitable framework to co-ordinate such functions and make them available as a *"package"*.

1.3.7 Policy and institutional reforms

Institutional reforms often follow policy reforms. Such initiatives may not require major investment activity *per sé*. However, good projects require good policy frameworks. The investment policy and institutional reforms are therefore important to optimize the impacts of development project types (1.3.1 – 1.3.6).

1.4   Why do Agricultural Projects Fail?

History records that agricultural projects implemented in most developing countries produce below the expectations. In Tanzania for example, the National Agriculture and Food Corporation (NAFCO) farms in Ruvu, Mbarali and Hanang failed in early 1980s despite heavy investments. What are the reasons for this? It may be that the project design was flawed or that implementation was at fault; it may be due to poor and inaccurate project analysis; or it may be due to unforeseen economic, natural or political changes.

A non-comprehensive list of *"why things went wrong"* may include the following:

- A lack of local ownership and responsibility, i.e. participative planning and implementation.
- Problems of project design and implementation.
- The use of inappropriate technology, cropping systems or animal husbandry.
- Inadequate or inappropriate infrastructure.
- A weak support system.
- Failure to appreciate the social and political environment.
- Administrative problems.
- Changing economic situations and market conditions.
- Externally driven project initiatives.
- Problems related to poor project analysis.
- Unrealistic expectations.
- Unsupportive policy environment.

1.5   The Future of the Project Approach

Participatory planning and implementation is one of the fundamental building blocks for sustained growth and change. The participation of the beneficiaries at all stages of the project cycle is critical to ensure success. The project planning format tends to accommodate such participation. With the proper attention to detail and with the elimination of the limitations listed above, projects should be viewed and could indeed be used as *"cutting edge"* for development in the agricultural and rural environment. This will, however, require a sourced policy and institutional framework.

CHAPTER TWO

Agricultural Project Management

2.1   Introduction

Projects are found in all sectors of the economy: in agriculture, industry, and even in service sectors such as tourism, education and public health (a project should not be confused with a programme and operations; *See* Box 2.1 and Table 2.1). *Agricultural project management refers to an agricultural investment activity upon which resources are expended to create capital assets that will produce benefits over an extended period of time, thus logically leading itself to planning, financing and implementation.*

Most people are familiar with activities referred to as "projects". One may think of the construction of a factory on the outskirts of a town, an irrigation scheme or a large farm. These are identifiable projects even by a layman. Some projects are, however, not easily noticeable: for example, a project to fight malaria in rural areas or a radio-broadcast campaign against HIV-AIDS.

A common feature of all projects, whether agricultural or not, is that they can be planned, financed and implemented. Therefore, the *costs and returns* of a project are known and they can be measured and counted in advance. For any project, the geographical location should be known and the people whom it intends to reach should be identified. The activities to be carried out and their financing are organized in sequences.

Box 2.1: The Difference between a Programme and a Project

The major difference between a project and a programme is not so much in the objectives stated, but lies more in the scope, the details, and accuracy. A project can be defined as a specific component of a broad programme. A programme is thus composed of a number of specific projects.

A project is designed with a high degree of precision and details in regards to its objectives, features, calculation of return and implementation plan. A programme, by contrast, generally lacks details and precision and aims at a broader goal often related to a sectoral policy of a country or departmental policy of an organization. Calculation of returns of a programme cannot be made since no details of activities or cost are provided.

From a development viewpoint, a programme looks more comprehensive because it can embrace a large sector of the economy, thus contributing in a more sensible way to increased national output, and having an important impact on the society.

Table 2.1: Projects vs. Operations

Projects	Operations
Unique	Repetitive
Finite	Eternal
Revolution change	Evolutionary change
Disequilibrium	Equilibrium
Unbalanced objectives	Balanced objectives
Transient resources	Stable resources
Flexibility	Stability
Effectiveness	Efficiency
Goals orientation	Roles orientation
Risk and uncertainty	Experience

2.2 Sources of Project Ideas

For every great agribusiness project idea, there are scores of others that just won't work. It is generally acknowledged that farmers can save a great deal of time, trouble and money by putting their ideas to the test before they try to implement them. Half an hour of careful thought, an afternoon of research or a phone conversation with a knowledgeable friend might steer away a flawed idea -- and months of wasted effort and thousands of shillings in losses.

Moreover, the process of testing your ideas will help to determine the criteria to take into account when creating agribusiness concept. Eventually, efforts will help lead to an idea that has a solid chance of success. Unlike giant corporations that invest huge sums of money to test potential toothpaste flavors or product names, farmers probably won't spend a lot of time or money to evaluate your ideas. What is important is to begin with these simple steps:

- **Demand based projects:** A demand-based project is one which satisfies a particular demand. In the agricultural sector for example, demand for a product is usually reflected in terms of consumer demand for agricultural products, export opportunities, and demand for agricultural inputs into agro-industry.
- **Need based projects:** Need based projects are an important element in development of different areas. Sometimes development may be promoted in relatively poor area as a means of increasing income earnings opportunities and poverty alleviation. Also, promotion of projects oriented toward particular target groups, such as women or under-privileged ethnic minorities, can also be need based, although such projects are usually expected to be self-sustaining.
- **Resource based projects:** Resources like raw materials available locally can be a source of a project idea. For example, availability of phosphate rock in Minjingu has propelled the building of a fertilizer plant.
- **Friends and associates:** If you know successful entrepreneurs, ask them what they think of your idea. Chances are they'll think of problems you are likely to encounter. You may be willing to face those obstacles, or you might decide that some of them are insurmountable.
- **Potential customers:** Their answers will help you focus on your potential market and will give you a sense of how strong that market is. Once you have some answers to these questions, you can begin to estimate your prospective potential revenues.

2.3 The Feasibility Study: Getting Down to Details

If your initial ideas and thinking could turn into positive results, begin work on a feasibility study. The study can take the form of a formal document that will help you recruit potential partners, investors or lenders. Alternatively, it can be a simple memo to yourself with a series of questions designed to help you decide whether you should proceed to the next level of commitment.

Either way, your feasibility study should address the following issues, each of which will require in-depth consideration.

- **The product or service**
  - What are the unique features of the product(s)?
  - In the case of non-agricultural products, how will it be designed, manufactured and delivered to customers?
  - Where and how will the product be cultivated?

- **The management team**
  - Does your team/family have experience in farming or the area of the project? What skills or qualifications are missing from the current team?

- **The market**
  - Who are the target customers? How big is the potential market? Is the market growing? What are the costs required to reach the target market?

- **The competition**
  - Who are your major competitors? Is your farm product or service superior to the competition? Would it be easy for competitors to duplicate your product or service? What are your competitors' strengths and weaknesses? How will competitors respond when your products enter their market?

- **The costs**
  - What will it cost to start and run your farm or project? Where will you raise the money from?

2.3.1 Analytical aspects of the project approach

A project is a clearer, distinct portion of a larger, less precisely defined programme. The project format is used to prepare and analyze a variety of agricultural investments and is an analytical tool for analyzing information on a consistent basis across the expected life or different phases of implementation initiative. The project approach to planning allows for comparison of several projects, or alternative designs of the same project, i.e. alternative options, thus making the resource allocation process efficient.

A major limitation of the project approach is its reliance on quality data estimates and projections and lack of participatory planning options. The project format is also only a partial analysis. The concept of project cycle and its various components are discussed below. A project, from its beginning to end, is recognized to pass through five stages. These stages constitute the Project Cycle (Figure 2.1).

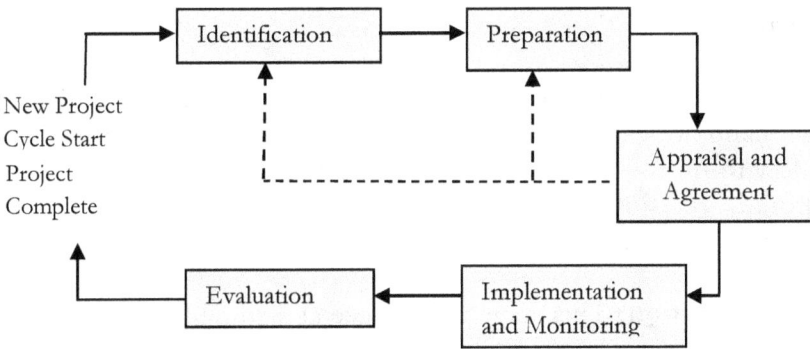

Figure 2.1: The Project Cycle

The activities within each of the five stages of the project cycle are summarized as follow:

Project identification: Here the project idea is translated into a preliminary description of the project. Terms of reference for the project reconnaissance team are established, and analyses of existing situations are made. These include a broad evaluation of the future 'with' and 'without' the project. The extents and limits of the project

31

are also proposed. Different approaches to the project are identified, and a judgment made regarding which option should be taken forward to the next stage

Project preparation: In this stage the project is designed. Objectives, prerequisites, inputs, outputs, organization, participants, clearances (administrative approvals by the government or the private client) are all defined, costs and earnings calculated, a financial plan is prepared, expected results are analyzed, the socio-economic and environmental impacts are estimated, and the provisional and final project documents are prepared.

Project appraisal and agreement: Appraisal documents are prepared and a succession of appraisal meetings, clearances, and financial negotiations take place. This brings the project to the point of meeting the required start-up agreement conditions, sometimes after revision and adaptation of project schedule, cost, objectives, and financing.

Project implementation: Here, the project management and lines of command are established and various implementation procedures laid down. In the course of implementation, project progress is monitored, revisions and adaptations are made for unexpected events, and finally the project is brought to completion.

Project evaluation: This stage takes place at a suitable time after the project has been implemented and project objectives, project implementation, and project benefits are appraised. This evaluation may result in the project being extended or in the identification of a new project, and may lead to the revision of methods by which similar projects will be formulated in the future.

There are other types of evaluation which may be carried out earlier in the project. These include project completion reports, which seek to identify problems which have arisen during implementation and which might have been unforeseen, and mid-term evaluations, which are characteristic of technical assistance projects.

Detailed sub-components in each project stage are summarized in Table 2.2.

Table 2.2: Stages of Project Appraisal

Project Identification		Project Preparation		Project Appraisal
Phase I	**Phase II**	**Phase III**	**Phase IV**	**Phase VI**
Preparation For Project Formulation	Reconnaissance, Preliminary and Project Design	Project Design Analysis Of Expected Results	Project Submission	Project Negotiation
Step 1 Project inception	Step 3 Analysis of the situation from an overall perspective	Step 7 Step 12 Detailed Financial, technical and economic analysis.Socio-economic investigations	Step 16 Project documentation and submission	Step 17 Project appraisal and negotiation
Step 2 Preparation of formulation work-plan				
	Step 4 Analysis of the situation having regard to the main interest groups involved	Step 8 Analysis and definition of project objectives,		
		Step 14 targets, and Social design criteria analysis		
		Step 9, Step 15 Design of Environmental individual impact analysis components		
	Step 5 Assessing the future without the project			
		Step 10 Design of project organization Structure		
	Step 6 Outline specification of a possible project			

2.4 Elements of Project Preparation

A properly appraised project is likely to attract investors and support from the government. From a developmental point of view, a soundly appraised project is often seen as some guarantee that resources will not be wasted if the project is financed. It should not be forgotten that, in many cases, resources to finance development projects are credits to be reimbursed in the future. These credits, together with accrued interests on them, are a heavy burden to developing countries.

In order to ease project implementation and to reduce the risks of debts resulting from project financing, the preparation should establish the project feasibility by means of an in-depth analysis of all its aspects. Knowing in detail how to analyze a project aspects in order to establish its viability, and consequently its acceptability, is of paramount importance.

Preparation for appraisal of a project - be it in agribusiness or other sectors is therefore a detailed analysis of the following:

- Technical aspects
- Financial aspects
- Commercial aspects
- Community participation
- Organization and management
- Socio-economic benefits
- Environmental impact
- Political risks
- Gender aspects
- Sustainability

2.4.1 The technical study

The technical study is a key area both in project design and in project appraisal. It analyzes the engineering of technical characteristics of the project including the design of construction and plants, the physical aspects of inputs and outputs, and the timetables for implementation. Major elements to be taken into account are project lay-out, technology use, equipment and civil engineering works. In an agro-processing factory project for instance, questions to be answered are:

- What are the dimensions and the characteristics of the building housing the plant in terms of floor area, height and storage capacity? (Bills of quantities and drawings should be produced).
- What are the specifications of the plant in terms of size, power, output, etc. (Drawings should be made).
- Are the water and power supplies adequate?
- What equipment or machinery and accessories are required and what are their specifications?
- What special skills are required to technically manage the project and how many skilled and unskilled workers are required at full capacity?
- What is the technology used and what benefits support its choice?
- What provision for maintenance or repair have been made?

The nature of the project will determine the type of know-how required to obtain an adequate technical study of a project. The aim is to show that the project will work as designed, provided that funds to purchase the required materials are available. The issue of availability of funds is dealt with in next the section on financial analysis.

2.4.2 Financial Analysis

The financial analysis of a project aims at demonstrating that the project will not be hindered by financial problems. The financial study establishes the magnitude of costs of investments, production and overhead. Investment costs include the costs for land development, technology, civil works, plant, equipment and consultancy. The production costs cover such items as materials, energy and labour.

Besides the cost estimates, the financial study will indicate possible financing sources including terms and conditions of credit. These refer to the type of loans, grants, or goods in a barter deal; the length of the grace or disbursement period; the level of interest rates; and the way the loan is linked to the purchase of goods.

The financial study is the basis for the working out of the budget requirement of the project. At the same time, an assessment of project outputs and returns will be made. These will be the basis for evaluating the project profitability.

Several methods for assessment of the project profitability are available. Although the most commonly used is the Internal Rate of Return (IRR), there are other methods including the Net Present Value (NPV), the Benefit-Cost Ratio (BCR)and the Payback Period(PBP)methods. Details of the use of these methods in financial appraisal are the subject of subsequent chapters, particularly Chapter 5.

Project profitability depends on a comparison of cost versus revenues using realistic prices of materials, labour and outputs. These prices are analyzed in the commercial analysis.

2.4.3 Commercial studies

The commercial study of a project deals with the analysis of the markets for inputs, materials, labour and products. The sources of inputs, their prices and the management of their supply is essential at this stage. Annual costs of materials, manufacturing, factory supplies, utilities, and agricultural inputs are estimated at this stage. The established price for inputs and outputs is then the basis for calculating projected income, future earnings, cash-flows and balance sheets.

The task of commercial appraisal is important because it enables the project planner to predict prices which are the basis for assessment of financial results. When appraising commercial aspects of a project, one problem often faced is the problem of prediction and forecast. In spite of modern forecasting techniques, projection of prices and yields/outputs remain a challenging task, requiring ample experience.

A mistake usually made, for example, is to over-estimate the production targets. Planners and politicians in developing countries are often too optimistic in setting project outputs. Assuming that everything will work perfectly is often taken for granted.

Unfortunately, in the environment of developing countries, there are many unknown factors that increase uncertainty: transport facilities are not reliable; supply of raw materials is irregular and not certain; unreliability of power; foreign exchange is insufficient to the extent that import of inputs, materials or capital items is often frustrating; managers are inefficient because of lack of incentives or adequate training; and farmers' knowledge in agricultural techniques is often insufficient, and extension services inadequate. Under such circumstances, optimism in target setting only leads to a waste of resources. As far as costing is concerned, it is advisable to use current prices and to include quantity and price contingencies. Sensitivity tests to check the effect of changes in prices, yields and outputs on project benefits, should also be done.

2.4.4 Community participation study

Participation analysis is often forgotten, even by experienced project planners. A participation study show what incentives are provided to project participants (the target group) in order to ensure that they successfully play their role in the project. This aspect is of principal importance in developing countries where communities are often requested to change their customs, or to contribute freely their labour force, or sometimes, their savings, in order to make a project successful.

Participants in a project can include farm families, project staff, input suppliers, government officials, politicians, workers' representatives and lenders. All the institutions whose collaboration in the project is required such as banks, consultants, firms, contractors and even villagers should be given a special treatment in project appraisal. But the most important of all project participants, and often the most forgotten by project experts, are the people sought to be involved in project implementation, especially in rural areas. These are often local communities who are generally the target groups expected to benefit from the designed project. This is where the challenging issue of community participation starts.

Recent experience of project implementation in developing countries has shown that successful projects are those which have been accepted and supported by local communities. They are projects which have obtained moral, physical and financial contributions from these communities. Individual firms achieve this through Corporate Social Responsibility (CSR). It is therefore an important assignment, for whoever is designing or promoting a project, to imagine strategies to ensure effective community participation in projects (See Box 2.2).

Box 2.2: Participation of Beneficiaries in Community Development Projects

Step One: Familiarization and networking

Once the project area is determined, people who have a mutual interest in the project are identified and a network is established to enable relationships between them. People involved include village leaders, local school teachers, religious leaders, members of producers or trading associations, village elders, influential men and women in local communities, and local experts. In this step, the data required for a preliminary analysis of the project is gathered.

Step Two: Identification of needs and priorities

Using local knowledge, an inventory of community needs is made. Classification and priority in satisfying these needs are established. At this stage, awareness of the problems and alternative ways of solving them are raised through seminars and campaign. Outside expertise is added at this stage.

Step Three: Agreement on priority needs and problem-solving methods

Through discussions and meetings guided by project experts, the project beneficiaries organized in a network agree on priority needs and on their participation in implementation of the project to be designed. This agreement includes methods of monitoring and evaluation, and form of contribution which might be money, materials, labour, attendance of meetings and involvement in monitoring.

Step Four: Detailed design of the project.

The project experts design the detailed project in which agreement of beneficiaries on project objectives, priority needs, chosen methods of problem-solving and agreed participation made, are included. The project organization chart should indicate the position of the project beneficiaries.

Step Five: Follow-up meetings and on-going evaluation.

During execution, regular meetings are held between participants and project management. The aim of these meetings is to monitor and evaluate together project implementation, and also to carry out education of beneficiaries on a continuous basis through seminars and campaigns.

The project appraisal report should therefore show how efficient and effective community participation will be obtained. It has been proven, for instance, that one way of letting the rural communities realize that they have a role to play in project implementation, is to involve them right from the start in the project planning process; that is, through all the steps of the project cycle. But more importantly, the key to success is to involve them in the identification of needs because a project is an answer to people's needs. Therefore, those who feel the need can best establish the priority projects for which they can give their moral support, their labour, their money or other contributions.

In rural projects such as rural water supply, crop value addition venture or rural housing, any project has a disrupting effect on the social life of the rural community. A well-planned project leads to the achievement of benefits to the target group. Since the negative effects of a project are expected to eventually be dwarfed by social benefits, it is generally accepted that programmes with relevant social benefits to communities should be implemented as a priority. But the attitude of the beneficiaries could be negative because of a lack of awareness of what is to be done. In this case, community development agents have an important role to play, namely, the one of educating the target group.

It is therefore advisable that the planning process of a project starts right from the community. It is also beneficial to the people that a project be *people centred* and not *technology centred*, especially in rural areas. In addition, the project planner should make sure that incentives are provided to people so that they find it attractive to contribute to project execution. This should be studied in project appraisal. Once strategies to ensure people's participation are planned, the problem of management and organization of projects becomes alleviated.

2.4.5 Project management and organization

Without adequate management and organization, no project can produce the expected results. It is thus essential that project appraisal makes a detailed analysis of project organization and management.
This analysis aims at answering the following questions:

- Is the organizational set-up of the project adequate?
- Will the project be provided with competent personnel to manage it?

- Is the local manpower market rich enough to provide the project with the required personnel?
- If the personnel is available on the local market, can competent staff be recruited freely?
- Should the staff be recruited locally or overseas?
- What are the implications of recruiting project manpower from foreign countries?

The right answers to these questions are the ones which will result in the assurance that the project will start as planned, will be satisfactorily implemented and will operate continuously after the project period. Even if the right staff is available, their success will depend mostly on the institutional set-up, that is, the relationship between various organizations involved with the implementing agency.

Appraising the project organization therefore includes appraisal of project-related institutions like subsidiary companies, cooperative unions, crop authorities, extension services, ministry headquarters, banks, transport companies and others. Some of the questions to be answered by such an appraisal are:

- What are the main regulations or procedures to follow in order to obtain the services required by the project?
- What are the policies that could become obstacles to project success, and which project design can alleviate this constraint?

When policies are too rigid, a policy change might be a condition for project viability. The project designer should investigate the acceptability of such a change.

2.4.6 Economic and social cost-benefit analysis

Economic analysis of a project aims at assessing the increasing wealth of the nation resulting from project implementation. When analyzing the economic and social benefits, the question to answer is: "Is the proposed project good from the viewpoint of national development interest?"

Methods have been developed to answer such a question. *Social cost-benefit analysis* is a technique which identifies the effects of the project on the economy as a whole by setting out and evaluating the social costs-benefits of investment projects. This comparison of costs and benefits helps to decide whether the project should be undertaken or not.

The aim is to measure the losses and the gains in economic welfare of the society in which a project is implemented. This raises several problems: first, the appropriate price of inputs and outputs; second, the valuation of the outputs of certain services; and third, the valuation of indirect effects called externalities.

In agribusiness projects, for example, a generally accepted advice is to use the farm-gate price for product output, the official exchange rate for foreign exchange, and the market prices. The unskilled labour price or the wage should be reduced or reasonably shadow-priced below the normal wage rate, while skilled labour should be shadow-priced above its wage to reflect its scarcity.

Besides the benefits offered by the project output e.g. crops produced, goods manufactured and revenues received, there are many other economic benefits of a project. The most obvious are employment, foreign exchange earnings, new technology and a better standard of living for the community served by the project.

2.4.7 Environmental impact assessment

Environmental impact assessment has become a common feature of project development in the world during the past decade. In most countries an environmental impact study is now a pre-requisite for project financing.

For example in the irrigation dam construction, we note that the scenic beauty may be spoiled and this becomes a *cost* because of reduction of pleasure enjoyed by the community before the scenery was destroyed. There has thus been an impact on the environment as a result of the construction of the dam. The environmental effect is a non-engineering, non-technical aspect that has recently gained momentum in project analysis.

Environmental impact of a project refers to the effect of a project on the world of animals, plants, water and humans existing in the project area. Most agribusiness projects carried out in developing countries do not even mention it. Yet these effects can sometimes be disastrous and the ecologist movement has increasingly made communities aware of possible disasters resulting from new projects.

Decision-makers should authorize only those projects which have no disastrous impact on the people intended to be served. This is the best way of ensuring, not only the protection of present targeted beneficiaries, but also of the survival of future generations. Twenty years ago, it was very rare for projects to be stopped for environmental reasons. However, in recent years it is becoming quite common.

A project planner must be aware that the authorities can refuse to give permission for implementation of a project. If a government stops a project, it is clear that this project is not politically feasible. Political feasibility should therefore be assessed by a thorough analysis of political risks attached to the project.

2.4.8 Political risk assessment

Appraising political risks is aimed at assessing trends in the political system and advising on the stability of the social environment. One rule is that agribusiness projects should not be encouraged whenever the government is unpredictable. The projects should only be promoted if large markets and the good economic opportunities exist. In addition, the project objective should not contradict government goals.

Most developing countries are characterized by unpredictable political changes. A change can be towards a dictatorship, a unique socialist regime or a multiparty democracy, or a blend of these. It is important to know that risks are omnipresent. In a new democracy, the risks result from the fact that the decision-making centre may change overnight.

A good project manager depends on more than one institution to act because businesses will be influenced by many groups like politicians, local governments, bureaucrats, opposition leaders, legislators, religious leaders, the media, the business community and the workers' union.

2.4.9 Gender question in development projects

The gender issue is now debated with a mix of animosity. Project planners should therefore take it into consideration. The expression *gender issue* is related to the concept of women in development. In this concept, the role of women in development is seen as being central. The strategy to involve women in the development process should generally cover all the steps in the project cycle.

The rationale for the importance of the concept of women in development lies first in the importance of women as a part of the total population of the community. Since the proportion of women of most communities is generally higher than that of men, it is accepted that no equitable community development will occur if the female component of a population is not included in project development.

The second aspect of the concept of women in development is the diversity of work traditionally and customarily performed by women: housekeeping, fuel wood collection, water fetching from distant sources, and cooking, are examples of daily chores assigned to women. These tasks consume time which could otherwise have been used more productively. Under present conditions in developing countries, work load, added to inadequate technology, often renders women inefficient and unable to participate fully in development activities. Yet women do involve themselves in production activities that yield a surplus.

In other words, , the reproductive function, added to the activities customarily assigned to women, are surplus activities for which other society groups like men or youth are not responsible. The concept of gender issue in development projects is justified by the general acceptance that women, as a disadvantaged group, should enjoy their basic human rights and therefore should not be subjected to any discrimination vis-à-vis men or any other group. Specific issues to consider in the design of a gender-balanced project are presented in Box 2.3.

Box 2.3: Checklist for Designing a Gender-Balanced Project

- *Involvement of women in project preparation.*
- *Access of women to land, water, food, shelter, education and health services.*
- *Access of women to income generating activities.*
- *Inequity in the distribution of resources to women versus men.*
- *Creation of jobs for women.*
- *Increase of the ratio of women labour in the total labour force.*
- *Increase of the ratio of women in the decision making body.*
- *Availability of activities specially designed for women.*
- *Increase of funds available for women's activities.*
- *Introduction of technologies which reduce women's workload.*
- *Impact on political equality between men and women.*
- *Influence of the project on the prevention of male abuse of power and violence.*
- *Education and training opportunities provided by the project to women.*
- *Influence of the project on the reduction of gender bias.*

2.4.10 Project sustainability analysis

Recently, the concept of project sustainability has become important among economists and planners. This concept is based on the belief that project implementation should result in benefits that have a lasting effect. Ideally, a project should not exhaust available resources like raw materials, inputs and skilled labour.

In this way, continuity in production of goods and services remains possible and project implementation does not consume all resources needed by future generations. There is now worldwide concern that the development we are seeking to bring about through project undertaking should meet the needs of the present, without jeopardizing the ability of future generations to meet their own needs. In sustainability analysis, the planner should make sure, therefore, that the proposed project meets specific conditions in respect of sustainability. Criteria for scoring project sustainability are indicated in Box 2.4.

Box 2.4: Criteria for Sustainable Projects

Low Cost: A project should only need a low investment cost.

Adaptation to Local Skills: A project should use skills which are easily obtainable locally, with or without special training.

Use of Local Raw Materials: A project should largely use local raw materials.

Output to Meet Basic Needs of Local People: The products or services of a sustainable project should meet the needs of the local beneficiaries.

Import-Substitution and Foreign Exchange Savings: A project should substitute imports and save foreign exchange.

Creation of Employment: A project should create new employment.

Profit Generation: A project should be profit generating or, should generate a surplus to make it self-reliant.

Environmental Harmony: A project should maintain environmental harmony.

Continuity of Production: A project should have a maintenance system which can allow its production process to continue even after financial and managerial support has ceased.

Supportive Institutions: A sustainable project should have plans to ensure the continuity of supportive institutions.

Gender Balance: A project should pay attention to women in development

CHAPTER THREE

Project Planning: Log-Frame Approach

3.1 Introduction

Participatory planning and development is one of the fundamental building blocks for sustained growth and change. The project identification process discussed in Chapter 2 underscores the importance of community participation in project formulation and implementation for its sustenance. Participatory project formulation and implementation is therefore *cutting edge* for development in the agricultural and rural environments.

Participation is a key to successful project planning. The Logical Framework Approach (LFA) is very useful in effective participative project planning. The concept and procedure of Logical Framework Analysis is discussed in this chapter.

3.2 Logical Framework Analysis (LFA)

The LFA approach is a tool for planning, monitoring and evaluating projects. This is also a useful approach to link projects (at the micro level) to the broader context of regional development programmes and national goals (i.e. the macro level).

LFA is essentially used as a tool to clarify cause-effect relationships and to clarify the logical link between project inputs and objectives; project activities and outputs; broader purposes; and the ultimate goals a project could serve. LFA is therefore a systematic planning process based on logical deductions.

3.3 The LFA Process

LFA is simply a planning tool that provides a structure for specifying the components of an activity or activities, and the logical linkages between a set of means and a set of ends. It places a project in its larger framework of objectives. It serves as a useful tool for defining inputs, time tables, assumptions for success, outputs and measurable indicators, or milestones, for monitoring and evaluating performance. It is a highly effective planning tool. In the following sections the LFA process will be described.

3.3.1 The project context

Before beginning to work on problem or opportunity identification, it must be clarified why we, individually or as a group, are going into the planning process and what the task is. It is therefore important to clarify the context of the project by answering the following questions:

- How can agricultural production be improved?
- How can farm incomes be stabilized?
- How can added value be generated?
- Who are the major stakeholders and beneficiaries?
- Who will benefit from the project and who will lose out?

3.3.2 The analytical phase

Analysis enables us to collect and analyze the data needed to plan the intervention. A range of groups are involved in development issues, such as the target group or groups, the national government, the regional authorities, the sponsor, the experts carrying out the surveys, the institution responsible for implementing the intervention and others. Each of these parties has its own angle on the situation or has some special contribution to make and they will all seek their point of view.

One method for analytical phase is to display the potential problems on a large chart. A check is made to see that all have understood them; if not, they are reformulated. The chart (which include negative statements perceived as problems) are displayed so as to highlight the cause-and-effect linkages between the different problems. This exercise will result in a problem tree (see Figure 3.1).

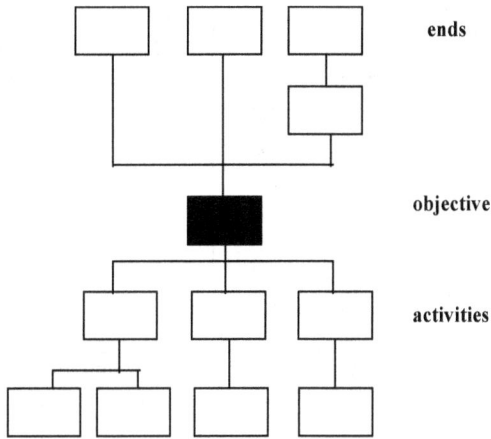

Figure 3.1: Developing the Problem Tree

By changing the negative states into positive states and by arranging these in groups reflecting the activity-ends linkages, the problem tree turns into an *objective tree* (see Figure 3.2).

If the participants accept that the activity and linkages are correct and complete, they will then, using the criteria at hand, carry out a *strategy analysis* and select the objectives which will constitute the bounds of the planned intervention. The analytical phase can break down into three stages namely:

(a) *Problem analysis (developing a problem tree):*

This is a methodological step which enables us to analyze an existing problem situation to identify the problems and put them into order and to highlight the cause and effect relationships in a diagram (problem tree) as outlined in Table 3.1.

Table 3.1: The Problem Analysis Process

Problem analysis $\longrightarrow$	Objectives analysis $\longrightarrow$	Strategy analysis $\longrightarrow$
Defining the ent		
Selecting the groups concerned.		
Analysing the existing negative states. (i.e.*the problems)*	Converting the negative states into achieved positive states: *the objectives.*	
Establishing a cause-and-effect linkage between problems.	Establishing resources-ends linkages between objectives.	
Constructing *the problem tree*	Constructing *the objective tree.*	Pinpointing groups of objectives to establish a coherent strategy. Comparing these groups using specific selection criteria. Choosing a group of objectives and purpose.

Steps for the problem analysis:

i.   Clarify the entity outlined.
ii.   Clarify the groups concerned by the entity (or sub-groups as the case may be).
iii.   Formulate the problems perceived by the groups concerned.

Lack of pesticides	Crop destroyed by vermin
Wrong !!	**Correct !!**
(less focus) (unfocussed)	(focussed)

For example:
(i)   Eliminate duplication charts.
(ii)   Check whether all charts are perfectly clear and reformulate them if not.

(iii)   Select a starting problem (a problem with causes and effects).
(iv)   Establish a diagram showing the cause-and-effect linkages between all the charts (the problem tree).

Notes:

- The problems identified must be real/existing problems or constraints, not imaginary or hypothetical problems.
- The importance of a problem does not depend on its position in the hierarchy on the problem tree.
- A problem is not the *absence of a solution* but *a negative state of affairs.*

An example of a problem tree is given in Figure 3.2. In this case problems are experienced with the transportation of produce (sugarcane) from a production site to the processing site.

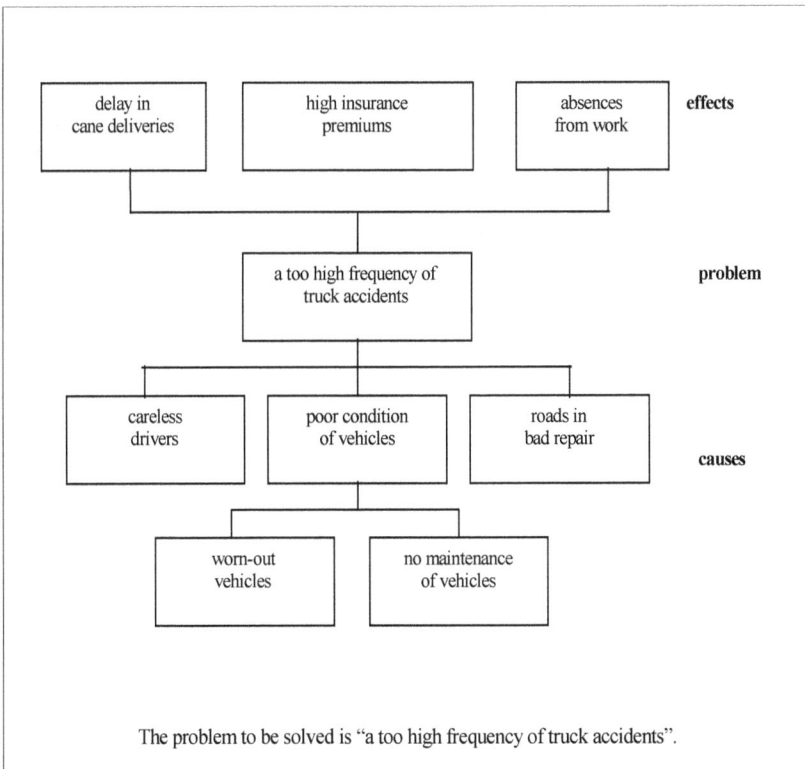

Figure 3.2: Example of a Problem Tree

(b) *Objectives analysis: The objective tree*

This is a methodological step which enables us to describe the future situation which will be achieved when the problems are solved, to identify the objectives and pinpoint their position in the hierarchy, and to show the activity-ends linkages in a diagram (the objectives tree).

Steps for objectives analysis:
  (i)   Formulate all the negative states in the problem tree to show them as positive states achieved in the future.
 (ii)   Check that the conversion of problems into objectives is realistic and acceptable from an ethical standpoint.
(iii)   Check that the "cause-and-effect" linkages have effectively turned into "activity-ends" relationships and that the diagram is both complete and valid. If not, adjust the logic.
(iv)   If necessary:
   • Change some of the formulations (to weed out nonsense or ethically debatable statements).
   • Eliminate objectives which are undesirable or unnecessary.

Table 3.2: Elements of objective analysis

What do we mean by objectives analysis?	Establishing resources-end linkages between positive states achieved in a targeted future situation
What does an objectives analysis look like?	It looks like a tree. The trunk is the core objective. The branches and twigs are "ends" and the roots are "resources".
Why do we make an objectives tree?	In order to obtain a clear overall picture of a targeted positive situation in the future.
Does the objectives tree show all possible solutions to given problems?	No. The objectives tree arises directly from the conversion of negative states into positive states, i.e. objectives. Hence the tree may not necessarily show all possible solutions to the problems in hand.
How do we change a problem into an objective?	The negative state is converted into an improved (positive) state which is achieved (projected into the future).
Can all problems be changed into objectives?	In principle, all problems can be changed into objectives. However, unrealistic objectives (i.e. enough rain) or ethically unacceptable objectives (i.e. all inhabitants to become Muslim) are not included in the objectives tree. In this case, the problem is reformulated and the objective will be correspondingly different.
What happens to "controversial" objectives?	"Controversial" objectives sometimes result from lack of understanding or poor formulation of the problems. In his case, the problem must be formulated more carefully so as to enable us to formulate an objective we can agree on. If the objective remains controversial, we drop it for the time being until we can bring fresh ideas to the subject. If the controversy continues and consensus proves impossible, the views of the different groups concerned must be shown together. A decision will be made as work progresses. Sometimes a controversial objective is shown in the objectives tree. It will probably become an assumption.

Note: The objectives must be expressed as a "state":

production increase	production increased

     Wrong !!   **Correct !!**

Not all "cause-and effect" linkages can automatically be changed into an "activity-ends" relationship.

(c) *Strategy analysis*

This is a stage which enables us to identify the different strategies possible to achieve the objectives and to select the strategy to be adopted by the intervention (or project) we are planning.

Steps for strategy analysis:
  (i)   Choose the goal, i.e. the objective to which several interventions will contribute.
 (ii)   Specify the activity-ends chains (intervention strategies) which will contribute to achieving the goal.
(iii)   Determine the most favourable and feasible chains, using, for example, the following criteria:
  - the availability of resources
  - the relevance of the purpose to the goal, its importance to the target group and the interest shown by the latter
  - the chances of success,- the link with development policy
  - the induced (i.e. unplanned) negative and positive effects
  - the time frame available
  - the degree of urgency
  - if necessary, the historical background of the intervention,
  - the ability of the local institutions which will be responsible for the intervention, etc.
 (iv)   Choose an activity-ends chain which will become the strategy of the future intervention, i.e. the major focus of the planned project.

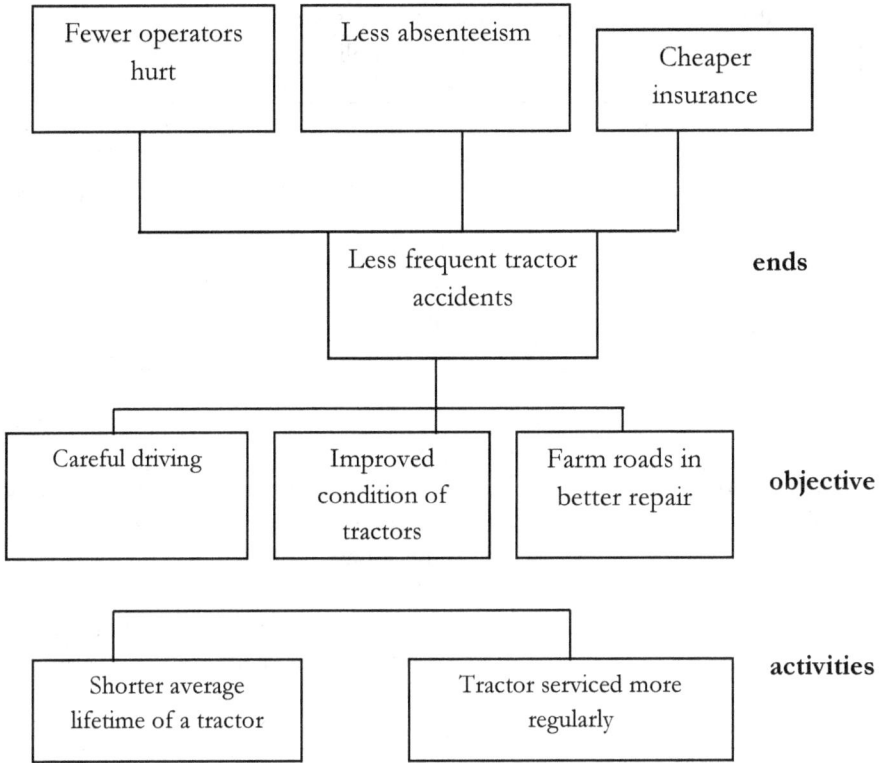

Figure 3.3: The constructed problem tree

Table 3.3: Elements of strategy analysis

What is strategy analysis?	It means pooling interlinked objectives to form an ensemble of objectives.
Why do we need strategy analysis?	Choices must be made since budget, time and other resources are not unlimited. That is why groups of objectives must be clearly specified and compared so that we may make a choice which will produce or achieve the purposes of the future intervention. We refer to a group of interlinked objectives as the "intervention strategy".
Is the choice of strategy a definitive one?	No. The chosen strategy is a first choice which may be adjusted, as the intervention becomes more operationalized.
What criteria do we use to make a choice?	The selection criteria differ from case to case: • Decision makers and development authorities apply general criteria as well as political and technical criteria; • Donor institutions/country should develop its own development policy and criteria for projects and programmes; • the target group has its own criteria; etc.
What happens to the objectives we reject?	If the groups concerned feel the rejected objectiveness is nevertheless important, they should be realized as part of another (or several other) parallel intervention(s).

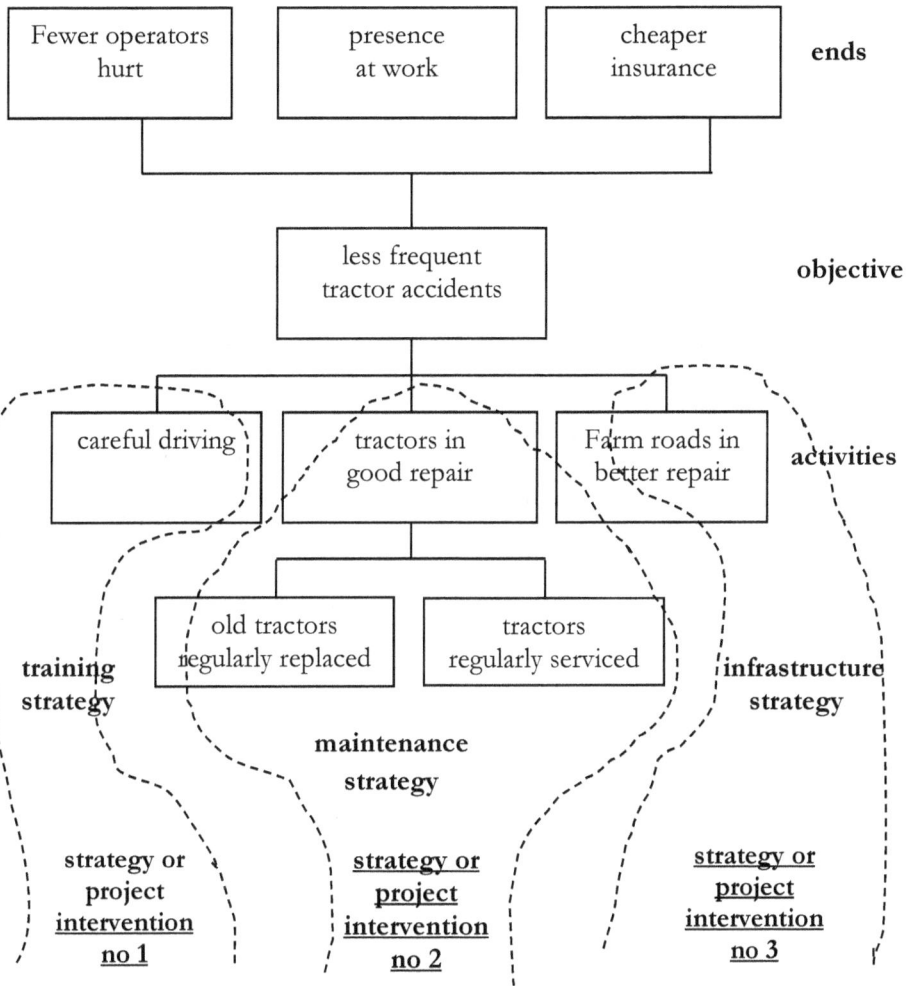

Figure 3.4: Example of a Strategy Analysis

3.3.3 The planning phase: Completing the log-frame matrix

(a) Describing the matrix

When we have analyzed the situation, the next step is to plan the intervention. The planning phase aims at setting up a logical framework (log-frame), in the form of a summary matrix showing four upright columns and four horizontal ones whose elements are described in Table 3.4 and exemplified in Figure 3.4.

Table 3.4: The Structural Components of the Log-frame Matrix

Columns			
Intervention Logic	Objectively Verifiable Indicators	Sources of verification	Assumptions
Goal			
Purpose			
Intermediate Results			
Activities	Resources	Cost	

Column one shows the (project) Intervention Logic (IL) which follows from the objectives tree. It is a summarizing narrative:

The *goal*: The future state at a high level, to which several interventions will contribute.

The *purpose* (or objective): The future state targeted by the project intervention itself.

The *intermediate results* (or outputs): The future intermediate states or outputs to be brought about by the intervention and which together aim at achieving the purpose. The (project) intervention leader is responsible for achieving intermediate results.

The *activities*: The work which must be carried out as part of the intervention in order to achieve the intermediate result. The intervention leader is responsible for carrying out and managing these activities.

Column two shows the Objectively Verifiable Indicators (OVI). These describe the goal, the purpose and the intermediate results in operational terms, i.e. in terms of quality, quantity, place and time. An indicator describes milestones of progress and enables detailed follow-up and monitoring. This column shows the *resources* needed to carry out the planned activities.

Column three shows the Sources of Verification. These indicate where and in what form information may be obtained in order to verify progress towards achieving the goal, the purpose and the intermediate results. This column also includes the *cost* of the resources needed to carry out the activities.

Column four shows assumptions: These are external factors over which the intervention has no direct control but which are nevertheless important with a view to achieving the intermediate results, the purpose and the goal. The intervention leader is not responsible for these assumptions but must bear them in mind, monitor them closely, take them into account and if possible, exert some influence over them.

The log-frame matrix summarizes the intervention in one (full) page as follow:

WHAT IS THE GOAL of the (project) intervention being carried out?

WHAT IS THE PURPOSE of the (project) intervention?

HOW does the intervention contribute to this objective (intermediate results)?

WHAT WILL the intervention DO (activities)?

WHICH crucially important external factors will determine the success of the intervention (assumptions)?

WHERE can we find the data needed to administer, monitor and evaluate the intervention (sources of verification)?

WHAT resources – and their cost – are involved in the intervention?

Description of the intervention logic

The intervention logic comprises all stages contained within the (project) intervention, which need to be completed in order to achieve the goal:

- intermediate results are achieved through the activities
- the purpose is realized through the intermediate results
- the goal is reached via the purpose

The following sequence is adhered to:

Description of important elements
What is the procedure for determining the intervention logic?

To identify the goal:

i. Study the objectives tree and select the objective situated at the head of a group of chains. This "objective" is now the goal. It is formulated as a positive state to be achieved; hence we should employ a past participle (see Figure 3.5).

Figure 3.5: Identification of a Goal in the Log-frame Process

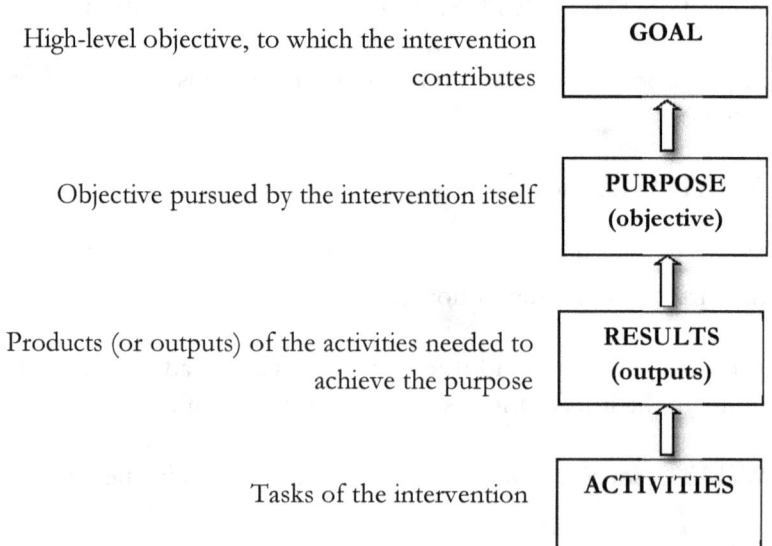

High-level objective, to which the intervention contributes — **GOAL**

Objective pursued by the intervention itself — **PURPOSE (objective)**

Products (or outputs) of the activities needed to achieve the purpose — **RESULTS (outputs)**

Tasks of the intervention — **ACTIVITIES**

To identify the purpose:

(i)   Study the objectives tree and select the objective situated at the head of the chain. This "objective" has now become the purpose. It is formulated as a positive state to be achieved; we should therefore employ a past participle.

(ii)   Study the objectives tree and select those objectives which, reasoning along "resource-ends" lines, will become intermediate results. These are formulated as positive states to be achieved; we should therefore use past participles.

To identify the results: If necessary, you should now add other intermediate results to achieve the purpose. These may have been identified by the groups concerned or supplied by technical staff.

To identify the activities: Study the objectives tree and select the objectives which, according to the resources-ends logic, will produce intermediate results. These objectives are now activities. They are formulated as steps to be taken, hence we should use verbs.

If necessary, you should now add other activities to achieve the intermediate results. These extra activities may have been identified by the groups concerned or suggested by technical staff. Number the activities and the intermediate results to create a logical sequence.

Define assumptions: Assumptions are factors not falling within the scope of the intervention which are not or barely affected by the intervention yet are important to bring it to a successful conclusion.

Table 3.5: Logics about Assumptions

Why do we introduce assumptions?	The intervention logic never quite tallies with reality. Factors not falling within the scope of the intervention exist and exert considerable influence. Just because they are outside does not mean we can ignore them. It is important to identify them and take them into account.
How important are assumptions?	Most interventions fail because of external factors relevant to the intervention. That is why it is important to investigate not only the intervention itself but also to understand the overall setting. If the external factors are negative, it may be preferable to drop the intervention altogether, or at any rate, redesign it.
Where do we find these external factors?	Some external factors are included as "objectives" in the objectives tree. Others are identified by experts or the groups concerned.
When do external factors become assumptions?	In the course of investigation, you should judge how important or even vital these external factors would be to the success of the intervention. If an external factor is important but does not fit into the intervention logic, it becomes an assumption and is integrated into the corresponding column in the log-frame.
How do we formulate assumptions?	Assumptions are formulated as achieved positive states. This means they can be verified and appraised.
At which level do we situate assumptions?	Assumptions link the different levels featured in the intervention logic. An assumption will therefore be situated at the appropriate level of the intervention logic. Choose the right level, and depend on the logic by linking the intermediate results, the purpose and the goal.
What use is an assumption at the upper level?	It indicates the factors outside the intervention which are needed to assure the planned impact of the intervention.
What is a "prior condition"?	A prior condition is a factor outside the scope of the intervention which must be achieved before intervention activities can get underway.

Steps for determining assumptions:

(i) Identify the objectives on the objectives tree not included within the intervention logic, yet important to its completion.
(ii) Situate these objectives at the appropriate level.
(iii) Identify the other external factors not featured on the objectives tree, yet necessary to the success of the intervention.
(iv) Carry out a check in three stages (at the three levels), starting with the activities of the intervention, to see whether the intervention logic is actually logical and comprehensive. At each level, you should bear in mind the external factors needed to reach the next level. If necessary, add more external factors to column four.
(v) Analyze the external factors identified in order and according to whether they can be integrated with the intervention logic depending on their chances of success or failure.
(vi) Depending on the outcome of your analysis
   a) Delete the external factor from column four.
   b) Insert the external factor as an assumption and formulate it as a positive state to be achieved.
   c) Redesign the intervention.

3.4 The Advantages of LFA as a Planning Tool

The LFA has the following advantages:
- It tries to make the project appraisal transparent by explicitly stating the assumptions underlying the analysis, and by allowing a check on the proposed hypotheses and expected results in an ex-post analysis;
- It deals explicitly with a multitude of social goals and does not require the reduction of the benefits into one figure;
- It is understandable to non-scientists. The log-frame, therefore, can be used as a tool to clarify trade-offs and thus, to ameliorate the decision-making process; and
- It is flexible with regard to information and skill requirements. It can incorporate social benefit – cost analysis, use input-output tables, and partial models. But it can also be used with

rudimentary information skills, albeit at the cost of more hypotheses and uncertainties.

Thus, a log-frame enables planners to:

- Set clear objectives
- Define indicators of success
* Set performance standards
* Incorporate change over time
- Clarify logical linkages in the plan
- Define critical assumptions underlying the project
- Identify key activity groups
- Identify means of verifying project accomplishments
- Define resources required for implementation
- Set up a need-based monitoring and evaluation system.

CHAPTER FOUR

Developing Agribusiness Cash Flow

4.1 Introduction

Understanding the concept of *cash flow* is of paramount importance in project planning. To grasp this notion, a clear definition of *costs* and *benefits* are needed first.

First of all, it is important to know the differences between two types of project analysis: financial analysis and economic analysis. In financial analysis, the concern is the point of view of a profit-seeking enterprise. In economic analysis, the interest is the benefits enjoyed by the society as a result of project undertaking. Generally, an investment proposal involves both benefits and costs during one or more time periods. It will therefore be convenient to estimate the value of the benefits and costs for each period, for instance, for each year. If for a specific period of time the benefits exceed expenditures, we speak of the net benefits or cash proceeds.

We undertake economic and financial analyses of agribusiness projects to compare costs with benefits from an efficiency viewpoint and determine which among alternative projects have an acceptable return. The costs and benefits of a proposed project therefore must be identified. Furthermore, once costs and benefits are known, they must be priced and their economic values determined and compared. All of this is obvious enough, but frequently it is tricky business.

In this chapter, knowledge about costs and benefits is explained with respect to the agricultural sector and how these can be defined, valued and compared in a consistent manner. These aspects are discussed in the following sections.

4.2 Identifying and Describing Project Costs and Benefits

4.2.1 Objectives, costs and benefits

In project analysis, the objectives of the analysis provide the standard against which costs and benefits are defined. A cost is anything that reduces an objective, and a benefit is anything that contributes to an objective.

The problem with such simplicity, however, is that each participant in a project has many objectives. For the farmer, a major objective of participating in a project is to maximize the amount his/her family has to live on. A farmer may have an objective to avoid risk and so may plan his cropping pattern to limit the risk of crop failure to an acceptable level or to reduce the risk of depending solely on the market for the food grains the family will consume. All these considerations affect a farmer's choice of cropping pattern and thus the income-generating capacity of the project. For private business firms or government corporations, a major objective is to maximize net income, yet both have significant objectives other than simply making the highest profit possible.

A society as a whole will have as a major objective to increase national income, but it clearly will have many significant additional objectives. One of the most important of these is income distribution. Another is simply to increase the number of productive job opportunities so that unemployment and poverty may be reduced, which may be different from the objective of income distribution itself. Any of these objectives might lead to the choice of a project that is not the alternative that would contribute most to income narrowly defined.

No formal analytical system for project analysis could possibly take into account all the various objectives of every participant in a project. Some selection will have to be made. For farms, we will take as the objective "maximizing the incremental net benefit" – the increased amount the farm family has to live on as a result of participating in the project.

For a private business firm or corporation in the public sector, we will take as the objective "maximizing the incremental net income and/or net worth". For the economic analysis conducted from the standpoint of the society as a whole, we will take as the objective "maximizing the contribution the project makes to the national income" – the value of all final goods and services produced during a particular period, generally a year. It is important to emphasize that taking the income a project will contribute to a society as the formal analytical criterion in economic analysis does not downgrade other objectives or preclude our consideration to them. Rather, we will simply treat consideration of other objectives as separate decisions.

Using this analytical system, we can judge which among alternative projects or alternative forms of a particular project will make an acceptable contribution to national income. This will enable us to recommend to those who must make the investment decision a project that has a high income-generating potential and also will make a significant contribution to other social objectives. Thus a multi-criteria analysis is often used to facilitate resource allocation.

In the system of economic analysis discussed here, anything that reduces national income (the objective) is a cost and anything that increases national income is a benefit. Since our objective is to increase the sum of all final goods and services, anything that directly reduced the total final goods and services is obviously a cost and anything that directly increases them is clearly a benefit.

4.2.2   Costs of agribusiness projects

In almost all project analyses, costs are easier to identify (and value) than benefits. In every instance of examining costs, we will be asking ourselves if the item reduces the net benefit of a farm or the net income of a firm (objectives in financial analysis), or the national income (objective in economic analysis).Major categories of costs encountered in projects are the costs of goods, services, labour and land. Cost items should always be assessed in quantitative terms.

- **Physical goods:** Rarely will physical goods or inputs used in an agricultural project be difficult to identify. For goods such as concrete for irrigation canals, civil works, fertilizer and pesticides for increasing production, or materials for the construction of homes in land settlement projects, it is not the identification that is difficult but the technical problems in planning and design associated with finding out how much will be needed and when.
- **Labour:** The labour component of agricultural projects will not be difficult to identify. From the highly skilled project manager to the farm worker maintaining the orchard while it is coming into production, the labour inputs raise less a question of what, than of how much and when. Although computerization is increasing, the human factor remains essential in all projects. There is no investment without labour in its broadest meaning; that is, the range of skills required from the unskilled worker to the highly

skilled manager. Valuation of skills can give headaches to the planner, especially in economic analysis where a shadow price is often found more appropriate than the market price of labour.

- **Land:** By the same reasoning, the land to be used for an agricultural project will not be difficult to identify. It generally is not difficult to determine where the land necessary for the project will be located and how much will be used. This factor of production causes a challenging problem of valuation. Valuation of land depends on many circumstances including land laws that determine its ownership and use. In agricultural projects, economic cost is based on the opportunity cost; that is, the net value of production foregone by investing in a new project. This is what project analysts call the *with and without* concept. Generally one of the following two methods can be used to cost land:
  o Direct monetary cost of land; and
  o Use of opportunity cost or net value of production foregone.

- **Contingency allowances:** In projects that involve a significant initial investment in civil works, the construction costs are generally estimated on the initial assumption that there will be no modifications in design that would necessitate changes in the physical work. In general, project cost estimates also assume that there will be no relative changes in domestic or international prices and no inflation during the investment period. It would clearly be unrealistic to rest project cost estimates only on these assumptions of perfect knowledge and complete price stability. Sound project planning require that provisions be made in advance for possible adverse changes in physical conditions or prices that would add to the baseline cost. Contingency allowances are thus included in a regular part of the project cost estimates.

- **Inflation**, however, poses a different problem. In project analysis, the most common means of dealing with inflation is to work in constant prices, on the assumption that all prices will be affected equally by any rise in the general price level. This permits valid comparisons among alternative projects. If inflation is expected to be significant, however, provision for its effects on project costs needs to be made in the project financing plan so that an adequate budget is obtained.

- **Taxes:** Recall that the payment of taxes, including duties and tariffs, is customarily treated as a cost in financial analysis but as a transfer payment in economic analysis. It is therefore not viewed as a cost in the economic analysis. The amount that would be deducted for taxes in the financial accounts remains in the economic analysis as part of the incremental net benefit and, thus, part of the new income generated by the project.

- **Debt service:** The same approach as above applies to debt service, the payment of interest and the repayment of capital. Both are treated as an outflow in financial analysis. In economic analysis, however, they are considered transfer payments and are omitted from the economic accounts.

- **Sunk costs:** Sunk costs are those costs incurred in the past upon which a proposed new investment will be based. These costs, however, cannot be accounted for in a Cost Benefit Analysis (CBA). When we analyze a proposed investment, we consider only future returns to future costs: expenditures in the past, or sunk costs, do therefore not appear in the analysis.

4.2.3 Direct and tangible benefits of agricultural projects

Direct and tangible benefits of agricultural projects can arise either from increased value of production or from reduced costs.

(i) Increased value of production:

This could occur in many ways.

- **Increased production:** Increased physical production is the most common benefit of agricultural projects. In a large proportion of agricultural projects the increased production will be marketed through commercial channels. In that case, identifying the benefit and finding a market price will probably not be too difficult, although there may be a problem in determining the correct value to use in the economic analysis.

In many agribusiness development projects, however, the benefits may include increased production consumed by the farm family itself.

The home-consumed production from the project increase the farm families' net benefit and the national income just as much as if it had been sold in the market. Indeed, we could think of the hypothetical case of a farmer selling his output and then buying it back. Since home-consumed production contributes to project objectives in the same way as marketed production, it is clearly part of the project benefits in both financial and economic analysis. Omitting home-consumed production will tend to make projects that produce commercial crops seem relatively high-yielding, and it could lead to a poor choice among alternative projects. Failure to include home-consumed production will also mean underestimating the return to agricultural investments relative to investments in other sectors of the economy.

Quality improvement: In some instances, the benefit from an agricultural project may take the form of an improvement in the quality of the product. Both increased production and quality improvement are most often expected in agricultural projects, although both may not always occur simultaneously. One word of caution: both the rate and the extent of the benefit from quality improvement can easily be overestimated.

Change in time of sale (time utility): In some agricultural projects, benefits will arise from improved marketing facilities that allow the product to be sold at a time when prices are more favourable.

Change in location of sale (place utility): Other projects may include investment in trucks and other transport equipment to carry products from the local area where prices are low to distant markets where prices are higher.

Changes in product form (grading and processing) (form utility): Projects involving agricultural processing industries expect benefits to arise from a change in the form of the agricultural product.

(ii) Reduced Cost

The various ways of reduction in costs of projects are discussed in the following sections:

Cost reduction through technology: The classic example of a benefit arising from cost reduction in agricultural projects is that gained by investment in agricultural machinery to reduce labour costs. Total production may not increase, but a benefit arises because the costs have been trimmed (provided, of course, that the gain is not offset by displaced labour that cannot be productively employed elsewhere).

Reduced transport costs: Cost reduction is a common source of benefit wherever transport is a factor. Better feeder roads or highways may reduce the cost of moving produce from the farm to the consumer. The benefit realized may be distributed among farmers, truckers and consumers.

Losses avoided: In discussing with-and-without comparisons in project analyses we note that in some projects the benefit may arise, not from increased production, but from a loss avoided. This kind of benefit stream is not always obvious, but it is one that the with-and-without test tends to point out clearly. This aspect may be critical for high valued perishable commodities.

(iii) Other kinds of tangible benefits

Although we have touched on the most common kinds of benefits from agricultural projects, those concerned with agricultural development will find other kinds of tangible and direct benefits most often in sectors other than agriculture. Transport projects are often very important for agricultural development. Benefits may arise not only from cost reduction, but from time savings, accident reduction, or development activities in areas newly accessible to markets. If new housing for farmers has been included among the costs of a project, as is often the case in land settlement and irrigation projects, then among the benefits will be an allowance for the rental value of the housing.

4.2.4   Secondary costs and benefits

Agribusiness projects can lead to benefits created or costs incurred outside the project itself. Economic analysis must take into account of these external, or secondary costs and benefits so they can be properly attributed to the project investment.

71

Instead of adding on secondary costs and benefits, one can either adjust the values used in economic analysis to account for the secondary costs and benefits in the analysis, thereby in effect converting them to direct costs and benefits. This is the approach taken in most project analyses.

Incorporating secondary costs or benefits in agribusiness project analysis can be viewed as an analytical device to account for the value added that arises outside the project but is a result of the project investment. In the analytical system every item is valued either at its opportunity cost or at a value determined by consumer's willingness to pay for the item through the use of shadow prices. By this means we attribute to the project investment all the value added that arises from it anywhere in the society. Hence, it is not necessary to add on the secondary costs and benefits separately; to do so would constitute double counting.

Although using shadow prices based on opportunity costs or willingness to pay greatly reduces the difficulty of dealing with secondary costs and benefits, there still remains many valuation problems related to goods and services not commonly traded in competitive markets.

Another group of secondary costs and benefits is often encountered in the "technological spill over" or "technological externalities." Adverse ecological effects are a common example and the side effects of irrigation developments are often cited as an illustrative example of this type. A dam may reduce river flow and lead to increased costs for dredging downstream. When these technological externalities are significant and can be identified and valued, they should be treated as a direct cost of the project or the cost of avoiding them should be included among the project costs.

4.2.5 Intangible costs and benefits

Almost every agricultural and agribusiness project has costs and benefits that are intangible. These may include creation of new job opportunities, better health, better nutrition, reduced incidence of waterborne disease as a result of improved rural water supplies, reduction of atmospheric pollution, green-house gas effects, national integration, or even national defense. Such intangible benefits are real and reflect true values. They do not, however, lend themselves to valuation. Because intangible benefits are a factor in project selection, it is important that they be carefully identified and, where at all possible, quantified, even though valuation is impossible.

4.3   Value Determination of Costs and Benefits

This section focuses on the calculation of values for costs and benefits. This will involve certain observations on scarce resources that can be used for the achievement of economic objectives and on the functioning of markets to determine prices of such resources.

4.3.1   Prices in cost-benefit analysis

Since resources are limited, an important consideration in their application is to find optimal combinations of resources through which the net benefit can be maximized. The value of inputs and outputs depends on a large degree to the level of sophistication of the economy in which prices are determined. Market prices (see Box 4.1) of products and services often do not reflect the actual economic value (scarcity value) of products and services, since government interferes in the operation of product and service markets through, for example, tariff protection, taxes or subsidies. To assess the economic effectiveness of the application of resources within projects, it is, as has been mentioned, essential that the prices of inputs and outputs indicate their scarcity (economic value).

Scarce resources are traded at specific prices, namely market prices. Provided certain conditions are met, market prices are the best criterion upon which the allocation of resources for specific uses can be based. The assumption is that markets are perfectly competitive and that supply and demand determines the prices of inputs and outputs. When the free operation of the markets is interfered with, for example, by the restriction or stimulation of either supply or demand or by price interference (through policy or market failure, or both), market prices do not reflect economic scarcity values and the use of shadow prices becomes necessary.

Box 4.1: The Various Valuation Terminologies Used in CBA

Valuation Terminologies

Valuation terminology: In valuing goods and services to prevent confusion, it is necessary to describe the terms used. In the literature on cost-benefit analysis the terms "shadow prices" and "accounting prices" have different interpretations. Terms in the cost-benefit literature related to shadow prices are defined below to prevent confusion. Although the terminology possibly may not coincide with that which the reader is familiar with, it is important to endeavour to ensure uniformity in concepts for the purpose of this book.

- **Market prices:** Market prices are those prices at which products and services actually trade, irrespective of interference in the market, i.e. the market wages of labour, the price of 2 kg of maize meal, the price of 1 kilowatt-hour of electricity, etc.

- **(Economic) Shadow prices:** Shadow prices are the opportunity costs of products and services when the market price, for whatever reason, does not reflect these costs, i.e. is distorted. Examples are shadow wages of labour, where the fact that minimum wages are fixed is taken into account; a shadow price for fuel, where taxes and subsidies are excluded; the marginal cost of generating 1 kilowatt-hour of electricity, where the cost of one kg fertilizer is subsidized; where the local price of an agricultural commodity such as sugar is artificially administered above the prevailing world market prices, etc.

- **Accounting prices:** Some writers use "social accounting prices", or "accounting prices" for short, as a substitute for the shadow price concept when a certain type of shadow price is referred to. In this book we use the term shadow prices to avoid any further confusion.

- **World prices (CIF. or FOB. prices):** The world price is the CIF (cost-insurance-freight included) price of imported or locally produced products or services that are internationally traded, or the FOB (free on board) price of exported products or services. These prices reflect the opportunity cost of products and services where the possibility of international trade exists. The CIF price of capital equipment and the FOB price of iron-ore or deciduous fruit are examples of world prices. It is important to consider the transport cost of imported products up to the point where the product is economically applied. The "world price" and "accounting price" concepts are essentially equivalent.

- **Shadow exchange rate:** The shadow exchange rate gives the value of the local currency relative to other currencies when there is no intervention in the foreign exchange market through, for example, the pegging of exchange rates or limits on capital flows. The shadow exchange rate is therefore the nominal exchange rate adjusted for the effect of interventions.

- **Surrogate prices:** Surrogate prices are used to value costs and benefits when no market prices exist or where no market price can be determined. Examples are the value of time and the value of a life. The prices can be determined with the aid of the willingness-to-pay principle. The price of, for example, clean air can be derived from what society (as represented by the State) is prepared to pay for combating air pollutions.

4.4   Determining the Values of Inputs and Outputs

Resources (or production means) are the scarce factors that are needed in the production process and that lead to the supply of goods and services by the private sector and government. The discussion that follows concentrates on general characteristics of means of production and the determination of the market prices and the shadow prices. These prices will be used to determine project benefits and costs.

4.4.1 Classification of inputs

During the production process project inputs are converted to outputs. The most important project inputs are capital, raw materials, labour and purchased inputs and services. Price information is usually available in market prices, but, as has been mentioned, the use of shadow prices is sometimes desirable.

Capital goods: Capital goods are those production inputs that are not used up in a single period in the production process. For the purpose of this book, they are divided into land, buildings and machinery, and transport equipment. Capital goods are usually viewed as the fixed assets used in the project. As such, capital goods, like any other product, are subject to imperfect market conditions which result in the market price not reflecting the relative scarcity of the product. Therefore it is necessary to investigate the valuation of these production means for such incorrectly determined prices.

Normally capital expenditure takes place at the beginning of a project. It may also, however, occur during the economic life of the project and in addition it may be necessary to replace capital goods during the life of the project.

Land: Land can be used in the economic process in a variety of ways, e.g. as agricultural land, an industrial input or the basis of infrastructure creation. The market price of a given piece of land cannot simply be accepted as a measure of its scarcity. The inherent value of land is dependent on its physical characteristics, the climate, and the production technology used on it. The shadow price of land is based on its opportunity cost, in other words the optimal alternative use to which it can be put. In order to calculate this price, the following information must be available:

(i)   The historical use of the land and the value of the output derived from it in the past;

(ii) Other developments in the area which can affect it; and

(iii) Information concerning the proposed use of the land and the output from the new alternative application.

It is important to remember that the expected return of any project is determined by prices reflecting interventions and imperfections in the economy over the duration of the project. Therefore, the expected return should be adjusted so that the economic value of the land can be calculated in terms of the economic value of the production in the optimal application.

An example can illustrate these ideas. The department of farm operations has to decide whether a tractor should be retained and upgraded or a new tractor purchased. An opportunity cost of zero (besides maintenance costs) is allocated to the existing feeder roads on the grounds that there are no other uses for roads and that their scrap value is zero. The land surrounding the farm, however, has alternative uses in the form of low quality agricultural land or housing plots, which must be taken into account as such. In the case of an agricultural project the "without project" use of the land should be used as the opportunity cost of land.

Buildings: Buildings are essential to protect the production process from the ravages of nature and as such are included in any cost-benefit analysis. In order to determine prices correctly, the following information may be useful:

(i)   The date on which the building was bought or built;

(ii) The current cost of an equivalent building and the book value of the building; and

(iii) Alternative applications of the building.

The shadow price of existing buildings is calculated on the opportunity-cost basis and that of new buildings on the basis of building costs. Where building costs serve as a basis for these calculations, adjustments have to be made for possible distorted labour prices which serve as an input, as well as for possible tariff protection on any locally purchased material inputs.

Machinery, equipment and transport equipment: Machinery and equipment are not usually used up immediately in the production process. Except where it is destroyed by natural phenomena or man-made disasters, the equipment becomes obsolete as a result of wear and tear and the availability of better production technologies. Depreciation on machinery and equipment is never, however, reflected directly in any cost-benefit analysis. Depreciation is taken into account indirectly in that the cost of fixed assets normally appears at the point when it is made, usually at the beginning of the analysis period and the scrap or residual value appears as a credit at the end.

The shadow price of machinery and equipment is determined in the same way as that of raw materials, by making a classification in terms of:

(i)   Machinery imported, with and without any restrictions on quantity and price.
(ii) Machinery purchased locally or made by the undertaker of the project.
(iii) Where equipment is leased or where machinery is carried over from other projects, the use value is adjusted for labour content, tariff protection, other indirect taxes and subsidies.

Raw Materials: Raw materials are found in a variety of forms and are converted through a variety of processes, by the addition of labour and capital, into goods and services. The opportunity cost (scarcity value) of a raw material, and consequently the shadow price of the raw material, depends on a number of factors:

(i)   Where a country is richly endowed with a raw material, but the raw material is a diminishing asset, e.g. coal, it cannot simply be accepted that the market price reflects the relative scarcity of the asset, since the government often influences the price for other reasons, e.g. in order to achieve a better balance of payments position.
(ii) Monopolies or cartels are in a position to force the price of the raw material artificially to a level higher than its scarcity value.

(iii) The subsidization or taxing of raw materials will distort the prices so that they no longer reflect scarcity values.

(iv) Rationing restricts the demand for or supply of certain goods and distorts the market prices so that economic value is not reflected in the price.

For a discussion of the shadow price of raw materials it is necessary to identify three possibilities:

(i) Where raw materials are imported without tariff protection or purchased locally, the market price, which by definition is the world price plus freight and insurance (CIF) to the point of consumption, is used in the economic analysis. In the case of quotas, which increase the price of the imported products on the local market, the same approach is used; in other words, the shadow price is equated to the CIF world price of the product. If government interferes with the operation of the currency market, however, adjustments should be made in the exchange rate.

(ii) Where raw materials on which import tariffs are applicable are imported or purchased locally, the shadow price is calculated by subtracting the percentage tariff protection from the local price. In the case of quotas the CIF world price approach is used.

(iii) Where raw materials are purchased locally and these raw materials are not normally traded overseas without influencing the local price or the local availability of the raw material (e.g. bricks), it can be accepted that the scarcity value or willingness-to-pay value of the product is reflected by its market price, adjusted for indirect taxes and subsidies.

Labour: Labour differs in many aspects from other production factors. In certain situations, for example, it is possible that there can simultaneously be a shortage of skilled labour and a surplus of semi-skilled and unskilled labour. At the same time factors exist in the labour market which result in the labour wage not reflecting relative scarcity one such factor is the fixing of minimum wages (through the pressure from trade unions or government policy), which forces the wage above the marginal product of labour and thus limits employment. All factors that cause the price of labour to deviate from the marginal product of labour should be considered in a cost-benefit analysis.

The following approach to determine the shadow price of labour is proposed:

Where unemployment does not exist, the market price of labour is used for all labourers. If the quality of a specific category of labour within a sector is homogeneous and the market operates fairly freely, then the average wage of the category concerned in that sector can be accepted as reflecting the market price in the sector. Under conditions of full employment, and especially where skilled labour is particularly scarce, this estimate will probably underestimate the opportunity cost of labour, but in the absence of specific information it is not normally possible to calculate it more accurately. Where unemployment exists, the shadow wage of semi-skilled and skilled workers (excluding professionals and managers) is based on the average minimum wage for the lowest paid workers in the industry concerned.

In general, it is unlikely that a lower shadow wage will apply, so that the possibility of over-estimating the opportunity cost of the labour involved is small. Even under conditions of unemployment, the labour of professionals and managers must still be valued at market prices, as normal market forces will largely influence wages for these categories. For a worker who has very poor technical skills and who lives in a region where unemployment exists, the average income per earner in the region is used as a measure of the production lost (shadow wage) when the worker is employed. Such income is usually lower than the minimum wage and is a more correct reflection of the opportunity cost of labour

Services: Purchased services are not always concrete or visible in the final product or service that is produced, but nevertheless form an integral part of the product or services, e.g. electricity, gas, water, transport and research and development. The opportunity cost of a service is the value that the rest of the economy has to forego if they are denied the service or the cost imposed on them to deliver the service. If, for example, a project needs electricity, the shadow price of the electricity in a given region will be equal to the long-term marginal cost of provision. The same approach applies to the cost of water, gas and transport.

Box 4.2: Principles of Evaluating Benefits and Costs

- *In valuing inputs, the opportunity cost of the resource in its most rewarding alternative use should be used:*
  - o *The input resource should not be undervalued for the purposes of the particular project;*

- *In valuing benefits, where the service provided by the project is not freely traded, more indirect methods of willingness to pay for the benefits need to be used:*
  - o *A variety of techniques are available to measure these values.*

4.4.2 Tradable and non-tradable goods

Cost-benefit analysis attempt to measure the efficiency which scarce resources are applied in the realization of a clearly defined set of objectives. Economic efficiency assumes that all goods and services are potentially tradable (directly and indirectly). All project inputs and outputs therefore have opportunity costs. Tradable goods can be defined by CIF (importable products) and FOB (exportable products) prices. Where a good is non-tradable the world market cannot be used to determine the opportunity cost. In such situations a good is viewed as non-tradable.

The terms tradable and non-tradable deal with the issue of tradability in principle – i.e. taking into consideration that comparative advantage and transport costs only.

A non-tradable good is defined as when:

CIF $\geq$ Local Cost of Production > FOB

A tradable good would be subject to one of the following conditions:

Importable good: CIF $\leq$ local production cost

Exportable good: FOB $\geq$ local production cost

The value of tradable goods will be determined by the "world price" (CIF or FOB).

Due to inflexibilities, labour and land goods are defined as non-tradable. Opportunity costs are used to determine shadow prices.

Traded and non-traded goods: The terms traded and non-traded goods are more practical as they take into consideration not only comparative advantage and transport costs, but also (expected) government policies on trade. Thus, a good which is tradable in principle may be non-traded in practice because there is expected to be an import ban on the good during the life of the project. A shadow price value assuming tradability may therefore be unrealistic.

First and second best shadow prices: A first best situation would be if all tradable goods would be traded. In such situations "first-best" shadow prices are used to calculate the economic values of project goods. However, if tradable goods are rendered non-traded due to policies or government interventions a more realistic value would be found in a "second-best" shadow price. In this system all non-traded goods are valued as non-tradables. "Willingness-to-pay" criteria will then be applied to determine the shadow value of non-tradables.

4.5 Dealing with Ownership Costs: Ownership costs have sometimes been termed as DIRTI. They are Depreciation, Interest, Repairs, Taxes and Insurance. Each of the five ownership costs is discussed below.

4.5.1 Depreciation

It does not make sense to charge the entire cost of newly constructed hog facilities, irrigation pump or a silage harvester in the year of purchase or construction. These assets are durable and provide a flow of productive services over time. Since durable assets can contribute to production over several production cycles, their costs should be charged out over the useful life of the asset.

Depreciation is a procedure for allocating the used up value of durable assets over the period they are owned by the business or until they are salvaged. By depreciating an asset, an allowance is made for the deterioration in the asset's value as a result of use (wear and tear), age, and obsolescence.

The proportion of the original cost to be depreciated in any one year is largely a matter of judgment and financial management. One aspect of financial management is the influence depreciation will have on income taxes. Another is the desire to have the underappreciated value of an asset reflect the resale value of that asset. That is, the depreciation allowance taken in any year would reflect the actual decline in value of the asset; thus the net worth statement would show the true value of depreciable assets.

What can be depreciated?

Depreciation can be claimed only on property used in your farm, trade, agribusiness or other income-producing activity. Examples are buildings, equipment, breeding stock, patents, and copyrights. Property is depreciable if:

- It is used in business to earn rent or royalty income
- It wears out, decays, gets used up, or becomes obsolete
- It has a determinable useful life of more than 1 year

Depreciable property can be tangible or intangible. Tangible property can be seen or touched, e.g., animals and machines. Copyrights and patents are examples of intangible property.

Depreciable property may also be real or personal. Real property is land and generally anything erected on, growing on, or attached to land. Equipment, tools, animals, and vehicles are examples of personal property. Land itself is never depreciable.

Treatment of Depreciation

As per accounting norms, the value of every fixed asset reduces over a period of time and this reduced value is calculated on an yearly basis. This decrement of original cost of the fixed asset is known as depreciation as per accounting forms. Since depreciation is a non-cash type of expenditure, a company can avail a tax benefit due to depreciation. The following basic conditions are required to be fulfilled for availing depreciation benefits:

- The assessee must be the owner of the asset. However, if the assessee is occupying any building as a tenant for the purpose of carrying out business, any capital expenditure incurred towards renovation, extension, etc. can be treated as the asset values belonging to the assessee and hence, depreciation may be claimed for the purpose of business income compilation.

- The assessee must use the asset for the purpose of carrying on his/her agribusiness.
- The asset must be used during the relevant previous year during which depreciation is being claimed. However, if an asset acquired during the year is put to use for less than 180 days during the year under consideration, then only the 50 per cent of the normal depreciation may be claimed.

The asset in respect of which depreciation is being claimed should fall within the eligible classification of assets.

Depreciation methods

There are three methods used in estimating depreciation of fixed assets. These methods are namely straight line method, sum of the year digit method, and diminishing balance method. These methods have been used extensively before 1981 and are commonly used to estimate annual fixed cost of assets ever since. The computing formula for each method is as follow:

Straight line methods of depreciation

This is a straight forward method in which the depreciation is obtained by taking the original cost of a fixed asset minus the salvage value and divided by the expected life of the fixed asset in the business.

$$O = \frac{OC - SV}{L}$$

Where;
OC = Original Cost or basis
SV = Salvage Value
L = Expected life of the asset in the business

Declining balance methods of depreciation

Depreciation in this approach is estimated by the following formula

$$D_d \quad = \quad RV \times R$$

Where;

RV = Undepreciated value of the asset at the start of the accounting period. In year 1; for example, $RV = OC$. In succeeding years $RV = [RV_1 - 1 - D_d - 1] \times R$ (salvage value is not deducted from original value before computing depreciation).

R = the depreciation rate. It may be up to twice the rate of decline, $1/L$, allowed under straight line method.

Sum of the years-digits method of depreciation

Finally, there is the sum of the year digit method, in which the formula takes the form of:

$$D_Y = \frac{RY}{S}(0C - SV)$$

RY=Estimated years of useful life remaining

S = Sum of the numbers representing years of useful life (i.e., for an asset with 5 years useful life, S would be $1 + 2 + 3 + 4 + 5 = 15$).

A comparison of the depreciation that would be taken with each of the three methods for $ 1,000 asset with an estimated 10 years' life and projected salvage value of 10 percent of the original cost is given below. The first three years' depreciation for each method would be computed as follows.

Examples

Straight line:

$$\text{Year 1: } D_s = \frac{OC - SV}{L} = \frac{\$1000 - \$100}{\$90} = 10$$

Year 2: $D_s = \dfrac{\$1000 - 100}{\$90} = 10$

Year3: $D_s = \dfrac{\$1000 \ - \$100}{\$90} = 10$

Declining balance:

Year 1: $D_d = R_V \times R = \$1000 \times 20\% = \$200$

Year 2: $D_d = (1000 \times 200) \times 20\% = \$160$

Year 3: $D_d = (800 - 160) \times 20\% = \$128$

Sum of the years-digits:

Year1: $D_Y. = \dfrac{RY(OC-SV)}{S} = \dfrac{10}{55}(1000-100)$

$\dfrac{10}{55}(900) = \$163.64$

Year 2: $D_Y = \dfrac{9}{55}(900) = \$147.27$

Year 3: $D_Y = \dfrac{8}{55}(900) = 130.91$

There are pluses and minuses for each of the depreciation methods. Straight line, for example, is simple to compute, and it preserves more depreciation for the last half of the life of an asset. This latter factor may be important in the tax considerations of a young farmer who expects taxable income to be rising over time, although with tax loss "carry forward" this is not a particularly big factor.

Declining balance depreciation is also attractive because many assets decline in value most rapidly during the early years of use. Several studies have shown farm machinery values to decline by 50 percent and more within four years of purchase. Certain other equipment, like automated feeding systems, may show even more rapid declines in value.

From Table 4.1 it should be obvious that, for assets held for the duration of their expected life, the total depreciation allowed is the same regardless of the method chosen.

85

Table 4.1 Comparison of Three Depreciation Techniques

Depreciation per year of new cost			
Year	Straight line (10%)	Declining balance (20%)	Sum of years digits
1	$ 90.00	$ 200.00	$ 163.64
2	90	160.00	147.27
3	90	128.00	130.91
4	90	102.40	114.54
5	90	81.92	98.18
'6	90	65.53	81.82
7	90		65.46
8	90	41.94	49.09
9	90	33.55	32.73
10	90	26.84	16.36
Total	900	892.61	900.00
Salvage value	100	107.39	100.00
	$1000.00	$1000.00	$1000.00

Source: Eberhard and Germann (1996)

In this system the numerator represents the useful remaining life of the machine and the denominator represents the sum of the number of years of life $(1+2+3+ \ldots + 10)$, or $\dfrac{10}{55}$ second year $\dfrac{9}{55}$; etc.

4.5.2 Interest

Money invested in durable assets is tied up and cannot be used for other purposes. This is true whether the money is borrowed or taken out of the firm's bank account. On borrowed money, there will be a regular interest payment, a standing obligation which must be met regardless of the use level of the asset purchased with the borrowed money. Likewise, an interest charge should be calculated on equity capital. In this case the charge would be an opportunity cost or opportunity interest. An annual charge should be made because the money invested has alternative productive uses, which may range from earning interest on a savings account to increasing production, e.g., income from acquiring several high quality dairy cows.

Annual fixed interest may be estimated by first computing average investment and then multiplying by an appropriate interest rate (r). One computing formula is:

$$\frac{(OC+SV/2)\,x\,r}{r}$$

Where:

OC = Original Cost of an asset
SV = Salvage Value
R = Interest rate

The reader will note that average investment is computed by *adding* original cost to salvage value and dividing by 2. Average investment is a middle value between the acquisition value and the estimated value remaining when the asset is either sold from the business, traded in on new equipment, or discarded because it is economically unproductive. An asset purchased new for $ 5,000 and scheduled for replacement in five years, when its projected worth will be $ 1,000, would have an average investment value of $ 3,000: ($ 5,000 + $ 1,000) /2 = $ 3,000.
The choice of interest rate, r, will likely depend upon the going interest rate on borrowed money and the rate of return expected from alternative investments in the agribusiness. If the best return expected for equity capital is interest on savings, then that should be used for. If there are several alternate investments with expected yields of 10, 15 and 20 percent, then an r of 15 or 20 percent should be used. An operator with limited financial resources would use the going interest rate on borrowed funds as the *minimum* value for r.

4.5.3 Repairs

It is customary to think of repairs as variable costs that depend upon the use level of an asset, that is, wear and tear. Most repair costs are variable costs. Some durable assets, however, deteriorate with time even though they are not used. Fences and buildings are prime examples, although they probably deteriorate even more rapidly with use. The same applies to hoses, belts, and some moving parts on machinery and equipment.
On some farm machinery, annual fixed repairs may average as much as 5 percent of new costs. Annual fixed repairs on buildings may be less than 1/2 of 1 percent. A busy agribusiness manager should spend time estimating fixed repairs on assets only where the value is expected to be large and should rely on estimates available

from planning manuals of management services or public agencies like the extension service for agribusiness professionals.

Some agribusiness managers prefer to include shelter as another fixed owners' cost. They recognize that if machinery is not housed, depreciation and maintenance costs will be higher. In some areas it is customary to include a fixed cost of 1 or 2 percent of new cost for machinery housing.

Some recent studies have shown housing to have some benefits, as well as the annual fixed costs. Trade-in value on five-year-old machinery that had been sheltered from the weather has been 10 to 25 percent greater than similar machinery that was left outside. Of course, this benefit is realized only if you trade in your machinery. However, the higher trade in value is a reason for not including shelter with the DIRTI 5.

4.5.4 Taxes and Insurance

Personal property taxes are levied on owned machinery in some countries. In other countries, only that machinery that is used for custom work is taxed. Real property taxes are paid on buildings. These taxes come due every year and, again, are unrelated to level of use or productive services provided. Any investment analysis that ignores the annual tax obligation associated with the proposed investment will be incomplete.

4.5.5 Insurance

Insurance too, is a fixed cost. Protection against fire, weather, theft, etc., may be required when a financed asset is purchased. That is, the lender may require the asset to be insured as a means of security for the loan. Some operators, particularly those with low equity, will want to insure some of their more valuable assets because of the strain the loss of those assets would place on the financial condition of the agribusiness. Other operators will self-insure; that is, they feel they can take risk and choose to do so rather than pay a premium to an insurance company to assume the risks for them.

4.6 Sources of Agribusiness Project Funds

Unless a farmer's net worth is sizeable, many farm assets are likely to be financed with credit. *Credit* refers to the ability to control the capital of another in return for a promise to repay it by a specific future date. The use of credit is constrained by the agribusiness' borrowing capacity. The *borrowing capacity*, determined by the lender, is the maximum amount of credit the agribusiness can obtain. However, the amount of credit to use, that is, money to borrow, within this constraint is a decision made by the farm manager.

The difference between the borrowing capacity and the amount borrowed is the *credit reserve*, a backup source of liquidity available for unforeseen events and investment opportunities. The credit reserve is the manager's unused borrowing capacity. For example, if a farm business has a borrowing capacity of $ 20,000 but borrows only 5,000, a credit reserve, or financial cushion, of $ 15,000 is left. The larger the reserve, the more able the farm manager is to assume risk. However, there is an opportunity cost associated with this credit reserve; this cost is the income foregone by not investing this capital in the agribusiness.

Any increase in borrowing, of course, reduces the credit reserve. However, by increasing the business' debt-carrying capacity, it is possible to increase the credit used from borrowing without necessarily reducing credit reserves. To increase the farm business' borrowing capacity, the agribusiness manager must be familiar with alternative sources of agricultural credit, understand loan terms and their implications, and approach the lender with a well-prepared presentation. These topics are discussed in the following section.

4.6.1 Classification of Agricultural Loans

Productive loans that a farmer requires, may be classified into short-, medium and long-term loans based on the length of the repayment period.

- **Short-term Loans:** These loans are generally advanced for the purchase of seeds, chemicals and hiring labour and machinery during a crop season. Short-term loans are, therefore, also called seasonal loans. The normal duration of such loans is generally up to 15 months.

- ***Medium-term Loans:*** These loans are advanced for financing the purchase of capital items the returns from which keep on accruing over more than one production period. Examples of such capital items are livestock, machinery and other farm equipment. These loans are generally expected to be repaid between 15 months and 5 years.

- ***Long-term Loans:*** Some assets like land, heavy machinery and buildings often need relatively large loans. It is normally very difficult for farmers to repay these huge loans in periods less than 5 years, particularly from the additional income generated by the asset. Such loans are normally expected to be repaid between 5 and 15 years and sometimes up to 20 years. In some countries, however, the repayment period may extend even beyond 20 years. For example, the long-term loans are contracted for a maximum period of 30, 33.5, 57, 63 and 75 years in Finland, New Zealand, Switzerland, Hungary and France respectively.

4.6.2 Sources of Farm Credit

There are many sources of farm credit available to an average farmer in most countries of the world. The best source of credit, however, depends on the amount and type of credit required and the preferences of the individual farmer to some extent. Some of the major sources of farm credit are the following:

(i) **Non-Institutional Sources**
- Relatives and friends
- Landlords
- Agricultural money lenders
- Professional money lenders
- Traders and commission agents
- Others

(ii) **Institutional Sources**
- Government
- Cooperatives

- Commercial banks, etc.

4.7 Basic Principles of Farm Finance

Financing the farm business involves a process of decision-making. How much to borrow, from which source to borrow, when to borrow etc., are a few important questions which every decision-maker has to answer before he or she decides to finance their farm business. As with the other decision making processes, economic principles are also used to arrive at judicious decisions from time to time. There are three basic considerations which must be borne in mind before a farmer decides to borrow or before a lending institution decides to lend i.e.

(i)   Returns from the investment
(ii) Repaying capacity and
(iii) Risk bearing ability

These are popularly known as the three R's of credit. If the additional returns from the use of the borrowed funds cover the principal and additional costs of borrowing and the borrower has sufficient capacity to repay the principal plus interest whenever it falls due and the borrower has enough ability to bear the risk and uncertainty arising from probable financial losses, there is a sound case for lending or borrowing. If the borrower fails to meet even a single criterion, the loan should not be advanced as there exists no economic basis to justify it. Sometimes the concept of the three C's (collateral, Character, Capacity) of credit is also used instead of the three R's, but basically both have the same requirements of credit analysis. The three C's of credit are character, capacity and capital position of the borrower. Loan should not be advanced until all the C's are favourable to a borrower. We will discuss here only the repaying capacity in detail.

4.7.1 Repayment Capacity

The repayment capacity is calculated separately for self-liquidating and non-liquidating loans. It is, however, essential to distinguish between self-liquidating and non-liquidating loans first. Self-liquidating loans are used for short-term purposes, i.e. purchase of goods and services which depreciate in a year or one production period: Contrary to this, the non-liquidating loans are used to acquire goods and services which are not directly consumed but are generally used over a period of time, thus they do not completely become a part of the costs of the first year.

The repaying capacities for each type of loan can be arrived at as follow:

(i) Repaying capacity for self-liquidating loans
= (Gross income) - (living expenses + working expenses excluding proposed loan + taxes + other loans and repayments due)
(ii) Repaying capacity for non-liquidating loans
= (Gross income) - (living expenses + working expenses including seasonal loans + taxes +other repayments due)

Example: Suppose an amount of $ 1,400 is to be used by a farmer as a self-liquidating loan. His repayment capacity with and without a loan may be analysed as below:

Table 4.2: Repayment Capacity with and without Credit

Loan variables ($)	Without credit	With Credit of $ 1,400
Gross returns	3,500	5,020
Working expenses	1,000	1,000
Returns over cash expenses ($)	2,500	4,020
Living expenses	2,000	2,000
Other loans and repayments due	400	400
Repaying capacity	*100*	1,620

It may thus be carefully noted from the above analysis that the repayment capacity has increased to $ 1,620 with credit from $ 100 only without credit. Almost always, the repayment capacity increases with the credit

92

4.7.2 Methods of repayment

There are several plans available to the borrower to repay the amount borrowed. The best plan, however, is the one which corresponds to the time and amount of repaying capacity. If the borrower has a repayment capacity of $ 1,000 and income accrues every six months, the repayment plan must include a provision of payment of $1,000 every six months. Any other repayment plan, like lumpsum repayment of $ 2,000 per year, would obviously be inferior. Some of the commonly used repayment methods for the long-term and medium-term loans are described in the following paragraphs.

Straight-end repayment or lump sum repayment

The entire loan is paid on the expiration of the term, however, the interest is paid each year. It has an advantage in that the requirement not to pay immediately may lead to capital formation. Also, when deep fluctuations in agricultural incomes occur from year to year due to risk and uncertainties, it may be a preferred method of repayment since instalment payment may not be possible during some years. All the same, this method has a defect in that lumpsum payment may be more difficult and the interest cost higher.

Amortized even repayment

According to this method, an equal amount is repaid each year. The amount paid includes two portions, i.e. a larger proportion of principal and a smaller portion of interest, in each succeeding instalment of payment as shown in Fig. 4.1a and Table 4.3. This method is preferred when income generated through the assets purchased with borrowed funds, like tractor and pumping set, is likely to be the same every year during the repayment period. The formula used for calculating the annual repayment of the loan according to this methods is:

$$SEP = PL\left[\frac{i(1+i)^n}{(1+i)^n - 1}\right]$$

Where:

SEP	=	Series of Equal Payments
PL	=	Principal Loan
I	=	Interest rate
n	=	Number of years for which loan is taken

Table 4.3 Amortized repayment

Instalment number	Amount of annual instalment ($)	Amount of Interest ($)	Amount of Principal ($)	Unpaid balance at the end of period ($)
1	263.80	100.00	163.80	836.20
2	263.80	83.62	130.18	656.02
3	263.80	65.62	198.20	457.82
4	263.80	45.78	218.02	239.80
5	263.80	23.98	239.82	-
Total	1,319.00	318.98	1,000.02	

Amortized Decreasing Repayment

Suppose someone has acquired US$ 10,000 loan payable for 10 years with 7% interest rate, according to this method, the amount of amortised payment remains constant every year (i.e. US$ 1420), but the amount of interest keeps on declining with every instalment of the repayment (Fig. 4.1b).

Amount of instalment ($)

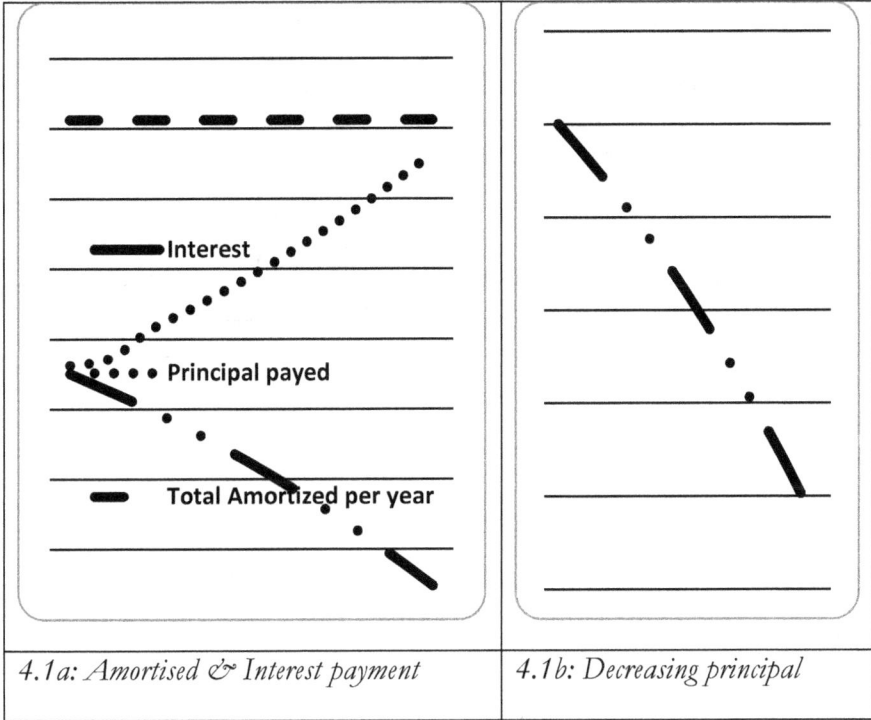

| 4.1a: *Amortised & Interest payment* | 4.1b: *Decreasing principal* |

Figure 4.1a & 1b: Amortized Even and Decreasing Repayment Plan

Thus, the amount of the instalment repaid becomes smaller every year (4.1b). This method is better suited for loans for the purchase of machinery and equipment on the farm as these items require lower amounts for repairs and maintenance during the initial year of their purchase thereby sparing more for repayment during these years. The decreasing repayment plan for the example in earlier section is given in Table 4.4.

Table 4.4: The Decreasing Repayment Plan

Annual amount of instalment number	Decreasing amount of instalment ($)	Plan amount of interest ($)	Amount of principal ($)	Unpaid balance ($)
1	300	100	200	800
2	280	80	200	600
3	260	60	200	400
4	240	40	200	200
5	220	20	200	-
Total	1,300	300	1000	.

Variable Repayment Plan

The defect with amortized repayment plans is that they are quite rigid and as such do not give any allowance to income variability over time. Thus the borrower may turn a defaulter during a year of low income. In order to get rid of this shortcoming, the method of variable repayment is sometimes suggested. Primarily, the agreements are made on the basis of some amortized repayment plan, but the loans are re-written every year taking into account the income variations from year to year. In years of good incomes higher amounts are repaid, while during poor years small, or no repayment is made.

4.8 Derivation of Cash Flow

Derivation of cash flows from the identified costs and benefits depends on whether the concern is that of financial profitability or of the effects on the whole economy.

If the costs exceed the benefits, we are dealing with *net expenditures* or cash *outlay*. The cash flow is the series of cash proceeds (or net benefits) and cash outlays (or net expenditures) associated with an investment. Table 4.5 gives a real-life example of projected project cash flow.

Table 4.5: Analysis of Projected Cash Flow over Project Period

Year	Fixed capital	Working capital	Operating capital	Financing cost	Total cost	Total revenue	Cash flow
1	(1457.35)	29.71	210.42	31.96	1729.44	544.37	(1185.07)
2	-	13.45	267.76	36.07	317.31	746.61	429.30
3	-	19.5	357.77	42.07	419.30	640.45	221.15
4	-	26.57	486.12	50.64	565.33	636.80	71.47
5	(445.37)	(91.22)	89.78	42.38	(404.43)	636.80	1041.23

One of the questions that can arise when analyzing a project is how to derive the cash flow, or in other terms, how to arrive at the values of benefits and costs, and the resulting gross profit and loss, starting from project data. The starting point for this derivation is the project assumptions, or, the conditions that must be realised in order to execute project activities. For instance, in an agricultural project, the planner may assume that the government will allocate 100 ha of land to a project and that 10 ha will be distributed to each farmer who agrees to participate in the project.

On the basis of project assumptions and data collected on the technical, social, economical and environmental aspects of the project, various parameters are quantitatively established. In a farming project, such parameters might include the quantity of output per unit area in kg/ha and the unit prices of inputs (wage in shillings per man/day, the price of one kilogram of fertilizer, the price of one litre of pesticides, and the cost of land development per hectare); on the basis of these parameters, it is easy to calculate the value of inputs and outputs.

The computed value of outputs represents the project benefits, and the value of inputs is the project costs. The same method of derivation is used to establish farm budgets.

CHAPTER FIVE

Techniques of Agribusinesss Project Analysis

5.1   Introduction

Farmers inevitably have to make investment decisions that can make or break their farming businesses. Having business acumen is not enough, however, knowledge of analytical tools to assist the farmer in investment decisions are critical. Investment is defined as an addition of intermediate and fixed assets to a business. Typical agribusiness investment falls into one of four major categories:

- Replacement of obsolete or worn capital items,
- Adoption of mechanized technology to reduce costs and increase profits,
- Expansion of existing enterprises,
- Addition of new enterprises.

Agro-investment decisions are particularly important to farmers because the effects are long lasting, as opposed to the effects of operating decisions such as feeding and fertilization, which last for only a short period of time. For example, if a dairy farmer finds that a ration chosen earlier is not appropriate, it can be changed. However, if the building constructed last year is not working out, it cannot be changed easily or without extra expenses. Investment decisions are usually costly to reverse.

Investment decisions are also important because the amount of money used to buy assets such as tractors, equipment, buildings, and land is expensive. These decisions are further complicated by the fact that large investment expenditures made now could generate returns over a long period of time, perhaps as many as 10 or even 20 years. It is difficult to predict what the returns to the investment will be into the future. Thus, the importance of these decisions justifies the use of a comprehensive method for analyzing their soundness. It is believed that time spent on a decision is often inversely proportional to the sum involved. Managers often lack the tools to evaluate these more complex and significant decisions. This chapter is meant to provide the reader a set of financial tools so that these analyses will be proportional to the importance of the decision.

5.2 Agribusiness Project Analysis: Different Analytical Viewpoints

(i) Financial analysis

Financial analyses focus on the business prospect of a project. The term "financial analysis" can, depending on the context in which it is used, refer to one or more accounting techniques, e.g. cash-flow analysis, profit determination, or the analysis of the source and application of funds. "Financial analysis" as used in this chapter refers to a cash-flow analysis from which present and future expenditure and income are calculated to determine the financial feasibility of a project. The analyses are done at market prices. In the case of public projects such analysis normally gives an indication of the pressure the project will place on fiscal requirements and the degree of subsidization it will require. Financial analysis is also called private analysis where costs and benefits are considered from an individual's or business' point of view.

Financial analysis is carried out for different purposes:

Assessment of financial impact: Financial effect to farmers, public and private firms and any other participating agencies must be assessed. For each, examine the current financial status against the projection of future financial performance.

- o Efficiency of resource use:
  - ➢ Return of project investment and repayment of loans capacity,
  - ➢ Profitability of individual enterprises.
- o Assessment of incentives:
  - ➢ Assess incentives for farmers, managers, and other participants and beneficiaries to participate,
  - ➢ For farmers, is incremental income enough to justify change?
  - ➢ For private firms, is it profitable enough for them to make the required investments?
  - ➢ For parastatals, is the return large enough to be self-financing?

o   Financial plans:
   ➢ Identify sources of funds, amount of funds, repayment timing, repayment terms and conditions of credit for individual entities, and
   ➢ Effect of inflation.
o   Financial contributions:
   ➢ Co-ordinate contributions from various sources and match investment requirements.
o   Assessment of financial management competence:
   ➢ Assessment of complexity of financial matters and therefore managerial requirements;
   ➢ Assess any changes in organization and management that are necessary and
   ➢ Identify any special training required.

Further, two important aspects of financial analysis are the farm budget analysis and the analysis required to reach a farm level investment decision.

o   Farm budget analysis is the beginning of financial analysis. The starting point of financial analysis usually involves representative farm models. Based on patterns of representative farms these models generate enterprise (crops and livestock) budgets to compare the situation "with-the-project" to that of "without-the-project". Farm budget analyses is static, i.e. one year and is useful to help improve management. In farm budget analysis:

   ➢ Current prices are used, depreciation included,
   ➢ Non-cash items are included, and
   ➢ Off-farm income is excluded.

Farm budgets, e.g. gross margin budgets are a useful starting point, but need to be adjusted, especially with respect to include depreciation. With adjusted budgets, it is easy to calculate real funds flow.

Farm investment analysis supports decisions to:

> ➤ Determine the attractiveness of investment;
> ➤ Use discounted cash flows;
> ➤ Determine dynamism of project over a lifetime ;and
> ➤ Include off farm income.

(ii)   Economic analysis

This analysis determines the economic efficiency of resource used in a project. By economic analysis it is meant that project benefits and costs are evaluated at prices which reflect the relative scarcity of inputs and outputs. The economic analyses normally follow the analysis of the source and application of productive funds, which is done at market prices. However, in economic analyses, prices used to value benefits and costs represent opportunity costs and reflect the actual economic value of inputs and outputs. The opportunity cost is the value of the best alternative application of an input or an output of the project. It also refers to a foregone economic activity as a result of the project. The market price of land, for example, does not necessarily reflect the opportunity cost of the land. Thus, when a price has to be determined, in the economic analysis for a piece of agricultural land used for maize farming but on which an airport is planned, the opportunity cost of the land is the discounted net output from the maize. Prices in economic analysis are referred to as "shadow prices".

(iii)   Social analysis

This analysis aims to determine the consequences of a project for the distribution of welfare. Welfare defines the effects of social factors such as equity and gender aspects on the overall benefits of the project.

5.3 Cost-benefit Analysis in the Public and Private Sectors

Important differences exist between cost-benefit analysis in the public sector (economic analysis) and profit determination in the private sector (financial analysis).The first difference is the fact that the private enterprise is concerned only with the interests of its owners or shareholders when profits are being calculated; while the public sector is concerned with the interests of society and the economy at large. With regard to the latter, a much wider spectrum of costs and benefits has to be considered than in the case of pure profit determination. Consider, for example, a new transport system linking an agricultural project to the market, which is cheaper and also provides transport for a part of the population, but entails environmental costs in the form of air and noise pollution. The associated summaries are presented in Table 5.1.

Table 5.1: Different Viewpoints and Dimensions of Project Analysis

FINANCIAL ANALYSIS (Business)_____	FISCAL ANALYSIS (Government)	ECONOMIC & SOCIAL COST-BENEFIT ANALYSIS(Society)
▪ Impact on those directly involved: farmers, financiers, project developers.	▪ Fiscal focus: outflows vs inflows (fares, etc.)	▪ Economic efficiency and distributional impacts.
▪ Decision criteria: financial profit, cash flow, equity.	▪ Tax (income)	▪ Shadow pricing.
▪ Market prices and direct impacts.	▪ Annual government budget criteria.	▪ Time periods: present vs future generations.
▪ Market interest rates, depreciation, tax, inflation, etc.	▪ Affordability and national priority.	

Economic and financial analyses differ in three important ways. Firstly, economic analysis would be ignored in the determination of profits in the private sector, but will be taken into account in a cost-benefit analysis as part of the cost that society must bear.

Next, cost-benefit analysis differs from profit determination in that all variables in the latter case are measured in terms of market prices, while the economic value and social benefits in the former case are often provided at subsidized prices so that the market prices of inputs and outputs, where they exist, are distorted and do not reflect the actual economic and/or opportunity costs and benefits. Because cost benefit analysis utilizes opportunity costs, market prices have to be adjusted to reflect the actual economic value of costs and benefits.

The third important difference between cost benefit analysis and the determination of profits as applied in the private sector, is in the rate used in the process where future benefits and costs are discounted to present value, i.e. the discount rate. While the discount rate in the case of profit determination is a market-related rate, which reflects the market cost of funds, as well as uncertainties and risk; the discount rate used in cost-benefit analysis represents the time preference of society and is referred to as the social time-preference rate. This rate is normally lower than the market-related rate. The most important differences between cost-benefit analysis in the public sector and profit determination in the private sector are summarized in Table 5.2.

Table: 5.2 Differences between Cost-Benefit Analysis (CBA) in the Public Sector and Profit Determination in the Private Sector

Nature of difference	Cost-benefit analysis (public sector)	Profit determination/financial analysis (private sector)
1. From the point of view	Community/society/Economy	Shareholder/Individuals
2. Objectives	Apply scarce resources effectively and economic efficiently	Maximize net value of firm – Private Profit
3. Discount rate	Social time-preference rate	Market rate or weighted marginal cost of capital plus uncertainty and risk premium
4. Value unit:	Opportunity cost	Market price
5. Dimensions	All aspects necessary for a rational decision	Limited to aspects of decision-making that may affect profits/losses of individuals
6. Externalities	Excluded	Included
7. Social impacts and intangibles	Excluded	Can be examined and weighed
8. Advantages	Additional goods, services, products, income and/or cost savings included in analysis	Only money income and profit determination
9. Disadvantages	Opportunity costs in terms of goods and services fore gone is difficult to determine accurately.	

Financial and economic values: Financial analysis of a project evaluates the project from a private investor's point of view. It aims to determine commercial profitability, and only inputs and outputs that enter this objective function are included in the calculation at prevailing market prices. Financial prices are the prices people actually pay and concern evaluation using domestic market prices expressed in domestic currency.

Economic analysis evaluates the benefits and costs of a project from society's point of view, which is what the government is concerned with. It presumes that commercial profitability may not adequately value the project from a social welfare point of view. Economic prices are the values that society would be willing to pay for a good or a service, and concerns the real net national income change valued at opportunity cost. Where economic distortions occur, financial and economic values will differ – in some cases quite considerably.

Divergences in financial and economic values can be attributed to various factors:

- Market "failure", due to monopolies, external economies, incomplete information, public and quasi-public goods, the paradox of thrift, and fallacies of composition.
- Government intervention or policy "failures" due to inappropriate, insufficient, or excessive interventions to correct market failures or interventions which disrupt otherwise efficiently functioning markets and causes distortions in markets and market prices. This generally involves two types of distortions: viz. **border** distortions, which include export subsidies and import bans, and the tendency to sustain an overvalued exchange rate; and **domestic** distortions such as direct subsidies and other interventions, which affect relationships among domestic prices.

5.4 Considerations and Application of Cost-benefit Analysis

Cost-benefit analysis (CBA) is aimed at assessing the costs and benefits of alternative investment projects or programme expenditures on a comparable basis as far as possible, especially through the use of a common value measuring instrument, namely prices that are determined on a consistent basis. In this way the problem of choosing between alternative projects is simplified since qualitative arguments for or against a certain project are backed up by numerical criteria. The central problem with cost-benefit analysis arises from the question of quantification.

The following aspects among others should be kept in mind when applying cost-benefit analysis:

(i) Framework of reference

Cost-benefit analysis, in reality, constitutes a particular conceptual model which can be viewed as an analytical model or framework of reference, which represents a simplified version of reality. Through the application of the framework the decision-maker is guided to think through the full repercussions of the investment decision. This prevents people from misunderstanding each other and thus increases the objectiveness and effectiveness of decision-making.

(ii) Pareto Principle

Cost-benefit analysis is a technique used in an attempt to bring about a more equitable allocation and distribution of scarce resources. The criterion in this case is the achievement of what is referred to as Pareto optimality, which indicates that at least one person in society is better off while no one is worse off. A necessary prerequisite here is that the social benefits of the proposed project should exceed the social cost. The central role that the Pareto principle plays is to ensure that CBA is aimed at distributional effectiveness. It should also be ensured that a given objective/goal is achieved with the application of the fewest resources possible by carrying out cost-effectiveness studies. Until now attempts to find a single criterion which covers all the essential aspects of importance in a decision on a project have not been very successful. Where possible, therefore, the Pareto criterion must continue to be supplemented with additional criteria and analyses. These include performance auditing, perception auditing, utility studies, impact studies, operational research and systems analysis, organizational analysis, sensitivity analysis, etc.

(iii) With and without comparisons

Project analysis attempts to identify and value the costs and benefits that will arise with the proposed project and to compare them with the situation as it would be without the project. The difference is the incremental net benefit arising from the project investment. This approach is not the same as comparing the situation before and after the project. The before-and-after comparison fails to account for changes in production that would occur without the project and thus lead to an erroneous statement of the benefits attributable to the project investment (see Figure 5.1)

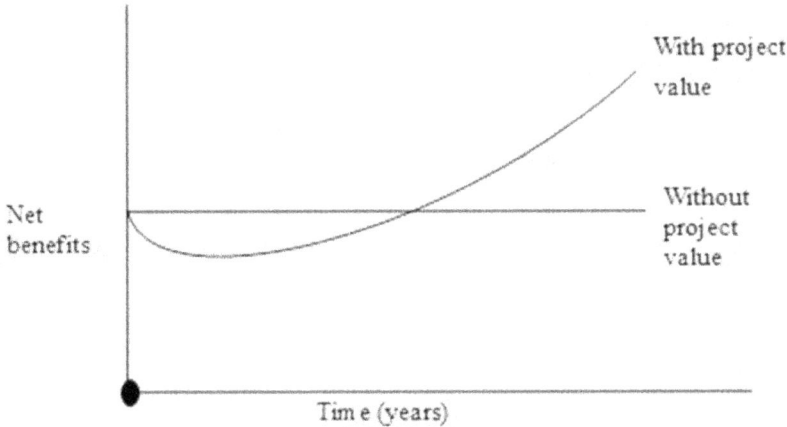

Figure 5.1: Schematic representation of with and without project situation

A change in output can also occur without the project if production would actually fall in the absence of new investment. The benefit from this project, then, is not increased production but avoiding the loss of agricultural output. A simple before-and-after comparison would fail to identify this benefit. The *without* project scenario would therefore require the same quality of preparation as the *with* project proposal.

A change in output can also occur without the project if production would actually fall in the absence of new investment. The benefit from this project, then, is not increased production but avoiding the loss of agricultural output. A simple before-and-after comparison would fail to identify this benefit. The without project scenario would therefore require the same quality of preparation as the with project proposal.

A change in output without the project can take place in two kinds of situations. The most common is when production in the area is already growing, if only slowly, and will probably continue to grow during the life of the project. The objective of the project is to increase growth by intensifying production. In this case, if the project analyst had simply compared the output before and after the project, he would have erroneously attributed the total increase in production to the project investment. Actually, what can be attributed to the project investment is

107

only the incremental increase in production that would have occurred anyway.

A change in output can also occur without the project if production would actually fall in the absence of new investment. The benefit from this project, then, is not increased production but avoiding the loss of agricultural output. A simple before-and-after comparison would fail to identify this benefit. The *without* project scenario would therefore require the same quality of preparation as the *with* project proposal.

(iv) Sensitivity analysis

Cost-benefit analysis is aimed at decision-making in respect of projects to be undertaken in the future and therefore involves projections and assumptions regarding future developments. This implies that an uncertainty boundary will necessarily exist affecting decisions in respect of the future taken on grounds of this methodology. It is therefore desirable that CBA should, where necessary, be supplemented by sensitivity analysis i.e. the analysis of risk and uncertainty, as well as additional information relating to these. The specific criteria used to rank alternative projects should be supplemented with sensitivity analysis to show the effect of possible alterations in chosen parameters.

(v)   Scope and focus of CBA

Cost-benefit analysis is not equally suitable for all projects and therefore it is important to clarify the type of expenditure programmes (current as well as capital) on which cost-benefit analysis can be performed. Many experts believe that CBA is particularly useful in the fields of agriculture, natural resource projects (i.e. irrigation), infrastructure and industrial development, but the latest studies indicate that it can be applied to almost any field. In those situations where CBA is not readily applicable, there is a need for cost-effectiveness analyses so that the decision-maker can be sure that objectives are achieved with the use of the minimum resources.   Even with the field of application clearly described, the information which the analysis provides is not always sufficient for the decision which has to be made in the public sector. This is because different national economic objectives of a strategic or political nature will not necessarily always be reconcilable.

In any CBA the ranking of alternative projects or programmes according to certain criteria must be supplemented with the results of all other analyses, apart from economic and social analyses, and all of these must as far as possible be quantitatively evaluated. In addition, qualitative analysis should be done where quantification is not possible. All the impacts and consequences of a project should thus be pointed out in sufficient detail to promote 'optimal' decisions concerning the project. At times quantitative analysis may reflect false accuracy. In the final analysis both objectives and subjective criteria should be used to make the decision. The qualitative analysis should complement the quantitative analysis.

(vi) Wider or secondary considerations

An important aspect of the application of CBA is that the wider or secondary economic impact of the projects under review outside the immediate sphere of influence of the project, i.e. factors such as consequences for the balance of payments or potential for employment creation, are left out of account or must be evaluated independently. In cases where such limitations apply to the field of influence, reference is made to CBA on the grounds of partial equilibrium analysis. On the other hand, the evaluation of the consequences, if significant, for the price levels, production or structure of large parts of the economy which lie outside the fields directly affected involves general equilibrium analysis as embodied, for example, in structural economic models, input-output models and semi-input-output models. Such models comprise comparisons which expose the relationships between key variables so that the effect of primary and secondary variations in a single variable against other variables can be determined. The model which is at the moment enjoying the most research and development attention is the input-output based Social Accounting Matrix model. The multipliers calculated from this model can also be used to provide indications of the linkage effects of projects. In this way, for example, the full consequences for the demographic structure, the labour force and distributional aspects of a development project can be studied.

Some analysts make these secondary consequences an integral part of the costs and benefits of the project and reflect them in the decision-making criteria of CBA. The desirability of this is questionable, and the multiplier effect should rather be shown separately to avoid any double counting. In the economic analysis, the evaluation of primary costs and benefits is sufficient mainly because opportunity costs to some extent already include the multiplier effects. Unfortunately, the boundaries between projects with negligibly small effects on macro-variables, which could readily be accommodated by opportunity costs; and projects which exert fundamental effects on such variables are often difficult to determine, and rational decisions depend on the sound judgment of the analyst.

(v) Data requirements

It must be emphasized that reliable statistics and a data base are very important to the implementation of a cost-benefit analysis. Generating such data may, however, be costly. In some situations a project below a certain cost value may not justify the cost of a comprehensive CBA.

From the above discussion it is clear that the methodology and an accurate application of CBA requires not only technical skill, but also a broad economic knowledge, profound insight and a clear-headed approach to problems. It is particularly important that the key aspects that are essential to the reaching of sound decisions should be separated from secondary information, of which note should also be taken. Exceptional expert knowledge, insight and experience are therefore needed for the successful application of the technique along with complementary methodology. In spite of the limitations mentioned, no single method normally provides more satisfactory results than cost-benefit analysis. Thus it has widely been used in decision making i.e. resources allocation among competing alternatives.

5.5 A Step-by-Step Approach to Cost Benefit Analysis

The CBA framework is designed to translate data and information into a financial analysis. After the financial analysis is completed, data is transformed into an economic analysis. The transformation is achieved by the following sequence of steps in the analysis:

Step 1: Specifying with and without situations

This step involves specification of with and without situations of the project to compare the additional benefit (if any) emanating from the introduced project.

Step 2: Estimating costs and benefits over time

Estimate physical consequences as benefits and costs over time in order to derive cash flows in the next step. Physical sources have to be identified in the form of physical inputs and outputs over time to cover the life of the project.

Start with a list of benefits and costs, and then estimate the quantities of each for each year. Important: please note that a separate list is required for the with and without situations.

Examples of benefits and costs of agricultural projects:

- Costs:
  o Physical production inputs,
  o Labour,
  o Land,
  o Contingency allowances,
  o Taxes, and
  o Debt service, interest on capital costs.

- Benefits:
  o Tangible benefits:
    ▪ Increased production,
    ▪ Improved quality,
    ▪ Time and location of sale,
    ▪ Processed products,
    ▪ Reduced costs (transport, machines) and
    ▪ Reduced loss.
  o Intangible benefits:
    ▪ New jobs created by the project.
    ▪ Better health, reduced mortality; and
    ▪ National integration.

Step 3: Value determination of costs and benefits

Applying prices to physical inputs and outputs in each time period, allows for derivation of benefits and costs. By deducting costs from benefits in each time period, net benefits are derived. This is done separately for the *with* and *without* situations.

Step 4: Discount incremental net benefit

Discount Incremental Net Benefits (INB) at the market rate. Market interest rates are used to discount INB to present values. Determine appropriate measures of project worth to assist in comparing benefits and costs by using net present value (NPV), internal rate of return (IRR), etc. These concepts are discussed in subsequent sections.

Table 5.3: Framework for determining Net Benefits

	Year 1	Year 2	Year 3	Year 4
Costs	$C_{11}, C_{21}, C_{31},$ ... C_{i1}	$C_{12}, C_{22}, C_{32},$ ... C_{i2}	$C_{13}, C_{23}, C_{33},$ ... C_{i3}	$C_{1n}, C_{2n}, C_{3n},$ ... C_{in}
Benefits	$B_{11}, B_{21}, B_{31},$ ... B_{i1}	$B_{12}, B_{22}, B_{32},$ ... B_{i2}	$B_{13}, B_{23}, B_{33},$ ... B_{i3}	$B_{1n}, B_{2n}, B_{3n},$ ... B_{in}
Net Benefits	$N_{11}, N_{21}, N_{31},$ N_{i1}	$N_{12}, N_{22}, N_{32},$ ... N_{i2}	$N_{13}, N_{23}, N_{33},$ N_{i3}	$N_{1n}, N_{2n}, N_{3n},$ N_{in}

Deduct net benefits *without* project from the benefits *with* project in order to derive annual incremental net benefits (INB).

Step 5: Transform financial analysis to economic analysis

Transform financial analysis to economic analysis by the following:

Step 5.1: Adjust for transfer payments. Deduct all taxes and loan service, and add all subsidies.

Step 5.2: Adjust unit prices of inputs and outputs so as to reflect social value. Shadow prices are used where market imperfections and government control results in prices that do not reflect opportunity cost and/or value to society. This usually applies to cost of land, labour, foreign exchange, and goods and services produced or provided under monopolistic conditions.

Step 5.3: Discount INB at the social rate. For economic analysis the social discount rate is applied, since market rates are usually higher than the social time preference rate. Derive appropriate measures of project worthiness such as NPV, IRR, etc.

Step 6: Conduct a Sensitivity analysis

To address risk and uncertainty, a sensitivity analysis is performed. The analysis involves adjusting values and prices of physical inputs and outputs on the basis of estimated probability of such variation, and redoing the whole analysis.

Step 7: Explore social impacts and intangibles

Social impacts include effects of the project on income distribution, social integration, employment, health, and nutrition. Such intangibles are usually not included in the analysis and calculations.

Step 8: Write up report to support decision-making

The whole analysis, including the sensitivity analysis, is written up to allow appraisal, review and decision-making by other professionals, decision-makers, and financiers.

5.6 The Time Value of Money

The methods for analyzing capital investments are based on the concept of the *time value of money*, which means that a shilling received today is valued more highly than a shilling received tomorrow or any time in the future. For example, in order to decide whether to buy a new tractor that will last for 10 years or a used tractor that will last for 5 years and will then be traded for another, a farmer must put a value on money to be spent and received in the future. Another example of a decision dependent on the time value of money is choosing to plant either an orchard that will not produce for several years or crops that will be harvested annually. The whole concept of time value of money lies on

113

a"cash flow" construct. Cash flow seems to be more important term than profit when it comes to understanding businesses. It is the slogan for current period of times. The value of money depends on when the cash flow occurs. Thus, the earlier value of money is greater than the latter one.

Why is a shilling received today worth more than a shilling received a year from now? If you lend someone $s.10,000 for one year, would you expect to receive just $$s..10,000 at the end of the year or would you expect to receive more? You would probably expect to receive the $10,000 plus another $1,000. The extra $$s..1,000 is compensation for the fact that $$s..10,000 received a year from now is not worth as much $10,000 today.

There are three reasons for the fact that a future payment is worth less than the same payment received today:

a) Opportunity cost

As a result of lending your money, you have foregone the possibility of earning returns from other investments. These other returns represent the opportunity cost, the shilling amount you could have earned if you had invested elsewhere. Money, like any other commodity, has a price. You can rent it or deposit in your bank and earn money or interest on that. The rent or interest on money is the investor's return, which reflects the time value of that money. It reflects a risk-free rate of return and rewards the foregone immediate consumption.

b) Risk

Because of misfortune or dishonesty, your borrower may not pay you back. The extra charge represents a reward for taking this risk.

c) Inflation

Assuming that there is price inflation in the economy during the lending period, the shillings that you get back will not buy as much as those you loaned. This decrease in purchasing power also justifies an additional charge. Under inflationary conditions, the value of money is expressed in terms of its purchasing power over goods and services.

Nominal or Market interest rate = Real rate of interest or return + Risk premiums + Expected rate of inflation.

Because of these three factors, a shilling today is not equal to a shilling tomorrow, a shilling 1 year from now, or a shilling 10 years from now. Comparing an investment that will yield $1,000 in a year to another that will yield $1,250 in three years is like comparing apples to oranges. To make these investment returns directly comparable, a common denominator is needed. Using the concept of the time value of money, the shillings from the two investments can be adjusted to their respective values at the same point in time. The basis of finding the time value of money is normally specified by the rate per period, denoted in percentage terms. Usually the chosen period is one year, more by convention than by rule.

There are two types of adjustments that can be made to determine the value of money at a given point in time: **compounding** and **discounting**. Compounding is used to find the value of the money at some future date when its present value is known. Discounting is used to find the value of the money today when its value at some future date is known. The time value of money is the major reason that banks and other lenders charge interest. Interest can be seen as the difference between the values of present and future shillings.

To understand the basic idea of time value of money, let us consider a venture that requires an immediate investment of $ 250 over the next 4years Table 5.3.

Table 5.4: Line of Above Cash Flows

Year	0	1	2	3	4
USD	-1,000	250	250	250	250

Cash flows occur at different points of time. For meaningful comparison, all these cash flows should be assessed at the same point of time. Either the cash flow occurring today has to be converted into its equivalent at a future date or the cash flow occurring later has to be converted back to today's value.

The future value of money that is available today can be calculated using the concept of compounding, referred to as future value (FV) or compounded value (CV) as shown in Table 5.5.

Table 5.5 Process of Compounding Value

Cash inflow in the beginning	Cash inflow in year 1	Cash inflow in year 2	Cash inflow in year 3	Cash inflow in year 4
-1000	250	350	250	250 FV(250) FV(350) FV(250) FV(-1000)

The present value of money accruing later is estimated by the process of discounting, which is known as present value (PV), as shown in Table 5.6. It is the inverse of compounding.

Table 5.6: Process of Discounting

Cash outflow in the beginning	Cash inflow in year 1	Cash inflow in year 2	Cash inflow in year 3	Cash inflow in year 4
-1000 +PV(250) +PV(350) +PV(250) +PV(250)	250	350	250	250

5.6.1 Compounding

Compounding is used to find the future value of a shilling amount when its present value is known. Compounding implies growth. If a sum of money is deposited in a savings account, it will grow until withdrawn. Suppose $1000 were invested in a savings account at 8 percent interest compounded annually. What would the value of this $1000 be after three years? The interest payments and balances for each year would be as follow:

Table 5.7: Compounding

Year	Balance at beginning of Year ($)	Annual *Interest* Earned (8%)	Balance at End of Year
1	1000.00	80.00	1080.00
2	1080.00	86.40	1166.40
3	1166.40	93.31	1259.71

The interest earned in the first year is 8% of the]$1000 ($80). The total value at the end of the first year is $s.1080 ($1000 + $80). In the second year, however, interest is also earned on the first year's interest; it compounds. The 8% multiplied by $1080 equals $86.40, which is added to the $1080 to give a value at the end of the second year of $1,166.40. This compounding process continues in the third year to give an ending value of $1,259.71.

The process of compounding to find future values is very tedious if many time periods are involved. The following formula can be used to simplify the process:

$$FV = PV \, (1+r)^n$$

Where,

FV = the future value, or the balance in the savings account at the end of n periods,

PV = the present value, or the amount originally deposited in the savings account,

r = the interest rate per period,

n = the number of periods (years, months, or days).

For this example:

$FV = \$1,000 \, (1+0.08)^3$

$= \$1,000 \, (1.2597)$

$= \$1,259.70$

The future value of a shilling depends on the length of time to that future date and the rate of interest that can be earned. These are the key variables in the compound formula for determining future value. The formula just presented can be easily executed on a pocket calculator, or the appropriate factor can be found in a table like that in Appendix 1. This table gives the future value of $1 at different rates of interest and for different numbers of periods. For example, the factor for three periods at 8% interest is 1.2597.

As indicated above, The FV of a sum of money invested at given annual rate of interest will depend on whether the interest is paid only on the original investment (simple interest), or whether it is calculated on the original investment plus accrued interest (compound interest). In the case of compound interest, there is a further factor affecting the future value, namely the frequency with which interest is paid (e.g. monthly, quarterly, or annually).

With simple interest, the future value is determined by

$FV_n = Vo_n(1 + r)^n$
Where,
   FV = future value at time n,
   Vo = original sum invested or the principal value,
   r = the interest rate per period

Suppose, you get a grant of $ 1,000,000 for your tomato processing firm from the Prime Minister's office. You find the money inadequate for immediate investment and decide to invest in a fixed-rate deposit at a commercial bank at the simple interest rate of 10% for 5 years. The future value will be the original of $ 1,000,000 plus 5 years interest, giving a total of $ 1,500,000. This is similar to the formula given above and applied below:

$FV_t = $ 1,000,000 [1 + (0,10)(5)] = $ 1,500,000.$

If r is the compound interest in subsequent year, the interest is paid on the original capital plus accrued interest. The process of compounding provides a convenient way of adjusting for the time value of money. An investment made now in the capital market of V gives rise to a cash flow of Vo (1 + r) after 2 years and so on. In general, FV invested today at a compound rate of interest i/Vo for n years will be:

$FV_{(r,n)} = Vo_{(1 + r)}$

Suppose an investment of $1,000,000 was put into building a cooperative society, paying a fixed 10% compound annual interest, what will the investment be worth after 5 years?

In a year's time, the investment will be worth
$1,000,000 (1+ 0.10)^1 = \$ 1,100,000$.

After 2 years it will be worth $1,000,000 (1 + 0.10)^2 = \$1,210,000$.

After 5 years, it will be worth $FV = 1,000,000 (1 + 0.10)^5 = \$1,610,000$.

Hence, the effect of compound interest yields much higher value than simple interest, which yielded $1,500,000. This is why fixed deposits in banks follow a compounded interest rate and yield a high return as compared to simple interest rate investments.

Changes in interest rates will concurrently change the value of money, which is also influenced by the period of time the money remains invested or borrowed.. The following example explains the effect of changes to interest rates.

Banks usually offer variable, rather than fixed rates of interest. Assume the rate to be 10% for the first 2 years, but it falls to 8% for the years 3 to 5. The calculation now has two elements:

$$FV_t =\$ 1,000,000 (1 + 0.10)^2 (1 +0.08)^2 = \$ 1,520,400.$$

If the interest rate remains 10% throughout 5 years, $FV = \$ 1,000,000 (1 +0.10)^5 = \$ 1,610,510)$. See how the future value of money changes with a change in interest rate. More frequent compounding of interest requires a change to our earlier example. Unless otherwise stated, it is always assumed that compounding or discounting is an annual process, making cash payments of benefits to arise either at the start or at the end of the year. Government bonds pay interest semi-annually or quarterly. Interest charted on credit cards is applied monthly. To compare the true costs or benefits of such financial instruments, it is necessary to determine the effective rate of interest termed Annual Percentage Rate (APR) or effective interest rate.

Returning to our earlier example of $ 1,000,000 invested for 5 years at 10% compound interest, we now assume 5% payable every 6 months.

119

The interest is $ 5,000 which is recalculated to give interest for the second half of the year or $ 5,200 for a total of $ 1,055,000 = 10/2%. The end-of-year value is, therefore, $ 1,060,200 (1,055,000 +5,200).

We can still use the compound interest formula but with r as the six monthly interest rate and n as the six-monthly, rather than annual, interval. In converting the annual compounding formula to another interest payment frequency, the trick is simply to divide the annual rate of interest r and multiply the time period n by the number of payments each year.

The generalized formula for the shorter compounding period is:

$$FVr = Vr/1+ k /m)$$

Where,
m = number of years compounding is done,
k = the nominal interest rate.

5.6.2 Discounting

An alternative way of assessing the worth of an investment is to invert the compounding process to give the present value of future cash flows. This process is called discounting. Today's value of any future cash flow is known as discounted or present value. It is the mathematical procedure for finding the present value of an amount of money when its future value is known. Discounting is the inverse of compounding.

When the choice is between $ 1,000 now and the same amount in one year's time, it is always preferable to take the $ 1,000 now because it could be invested over the next year at, say, a 10% interest rate to produce $ 1,100. If 10% is the best available annual rate of interest, then one would be indifferent to receive $ 1,000 now or $ 1,100 after one year. Hence, the present value of $ 1,100 received after one year is $ 1,000.

We can obtain present value simply by dividing the future cash flow by 1 plus the rate of interest:.

$$FV = \frac{Tshs.\,1100}{(1+0.10)} = \frac{Tshs.\,1100}{(1.1)} = Tshs\ 1000$$

Referring back to the savings account example, find the present value of $1,259.70 to be received at the end of three years, assuming 8% interest compounded annually. The present value is $1000 which is the quantity of money that would have been deposited or invested today at 8% compound interest to realize $1259.70 after three years.

Recall that earlier we specified the future value as:

$$FV_n = Vo(1 + r)^n$$

Divide both sides by $(1+ r)^n$ to obtain the following:

$$\text{Present value} = \frac{FV_n}{(1+0.10)} = PV_n$$

Now suppose a manager is interested in the present value of a coconut trees that will be ready for market in eight years at a value of $$s..10,000. The current interest rate is 10 percent. To find the present value of money to be received or paid at some future time, the following formula is used:

$$PV = FV/(1+r)^n$$

The definitions of these terms (PV, FV, r, and n) are the same as for compounding, except that here the manager is solving for the present value, PV. For this example, the calculations are as follows:

$$PV = \$\ 10,000/\ (1\ \ + 0.10)^8$$
$$= \$10,000/\ (2.1436)$$
$$= \$4,665$$

If it will cost no more than $4,665 to plant the coconut trees today and there will be no other costs later, then this investment alternative will be profitable. It may not be the most profitable alternative, but it is profitable in providing at least a 10 percent rate of return. Again, factors are available to simplify the calculations (see Appendix 1). The factor for eight years and 10% interest is 0.4665. Multiplying this factor by $10,000 gives the same result as calculated previously:

$$PV = \$10,000 \times 0.665 = \$4,665$$

Note that this factor is the inverse of the compounding factor for eight years and 10% as found in Appendix l.

As with compounding, discounting is also effected by changing financial market conditions and time periods. It is useful to see how the discounting process affects present values at different rates of interest. It can be seen in Table 5.7 that the value of $ 1 decreased very significantly as the rate and period increases from 0 to 20% and within 10 years, respectively. Table 5.8 summarizes the discount factor for three rates of interest. Investment surveys (e.g. Pike 1988) suggest that a 15% discount rate is the most popular and useful discount rate used in evaluation of capital projects. In this case, the discounted value approximately halves every 5 years. Thus, the value of $ 1 is 50 cents after 5 years, 25 cents after 10 years, and so on.

Table 5.8: Effect of Interest Rates and Time Periods

Year	*10%*	*15%*	*20%*
0	1.0	1.0	1.0
5	0.6	0.5	0.4
10	0.4	0.25	0.16
15	0..24	0.12	0.06
20	0.15	0.06	0.03
25	0.19	0.03	0.01

Table 5.9: Discount Factor

Year					%
0.10					
0.75					5
0.50					10
0.25					15
0.00					20
Period (year)	2	4	6	8	10

Discount table and present value: Much of the medium of using formulae and power functions can be eased by using discount tables or computer-based spreadsheet packages. The discount factor or interest factor i.e. 1 for a 10% discount rate in 3 years time is:

$$1/(1.10)^3 = 0.751$$

This can be found in Appendix 1 by locating the 10% column and the 3 years row. We call this the present value interest factor (PVIF) and express it as $PVIF_{(10\%-3years)}$ or $PVIF_{(10=3)}$.

$$PVIF_{(r,n)} = 1/(1 + r)^n$$

$$PV_n = \text{Present value} = \frac{'FV_n}{(1 + r)^n} = FV_n = PVIF_{r,n}$$

Hence, the present value of a future sum can be estimated by determining the PVIF for the given values of 1 and n. The factor value needs to be multiplied by the given sum. The PVIF value cannot be greater than one as PVIF (i, n) is the present value of 1 that will be received after n years at a rate of interest i%. The PVIF values for different combinations of i and n are given in Appendix 1.

Compounded table and future formulae:

The inverse of PVIF is the future value interest factor (FVIF) and is written as follows:

$$PV_n = \text{Present value} = \frac{FV_n}{(1 + r)^n} = FV_n = PVIF_{(r,n)}$$

Therefore, the compounded value of the future value is written as:

$$FV_n = PV_n (1 + r)^n$$

$$PV_n + FVIF_{(1,n)}$$

$PVIF(i,n) = (1 + r)^n$

Therefore, $PVIF_{(r,n)} = 1/FVIF_{(r,n)}$

The FVIF values for different combinations of r and n are given in Appendix 1.

5.6.3 Annuity

Annuity is an investment paying a fixed sum "A" each year for a specified period of time *n* at the rate of interest i. It is applicable in the case of a series of periodic receipts or payments. The equal amount of payment or receipt is known as annuity. Examples of annuities include many credit agreements and house mortgages.

Present value of an annuity

The present value of a regular annual receipts can be represented in terms of the symbols defined as follows:

$$PVA_n = A/(1 + r) + A/(1 + r)^2 + A/(1 + r)^3 + \ldots + A/(1 + r)^n \ldots (5.1)$$

Multiplying both sides by $(1 + r)^n$, we get,

$$PVA_n(1 + r) = A + A/(1 + r) + A/(1 + AV + \ldots + A(1 = r)^{n=r} \ldots (5.2)$$

Subtracting equation 5.1 from equation 5.2.we get,

$$PVA_{nr} = A - A/(1 + r)^n = A(1 - 1/(1 + r)^n \ldots (5.3)$$

$$PVA_n = A \left| \frac{(1+r)^n - 1}{r(1+r)^n} \right| = A + PVIFA_{(r,n)}$$

The $PVIFA_{(r,n)}$ values for different combinations of r and *n* are given in Appendix 1.

To understand it better look at the following example:

Suppose an annuity of $ 1000 is issued for 20 years at 10%. Using Tables in Appendix 1, we can find the present value as follow:

$$PVA_{(10, 20)} = \$ 1,000 = PVIFA_{(10,20)} = \$ 1,000 = 8.5186 =$$

$ 8.518.60.

Future values of an annuity

The future value of a regular annuity can be expressed as follows:

$$FVA = A(1 + r)^{n-1} + A(1 + r)^{n-2} \dots.. A\dots..(5.4)$$

Multiplying Equation (5.4) by $(1 + r)$ on both sides, we get

$$PVA(1 + r)^{n} + A(1 + r)^{n-1} + \underline{\quad\quad} (1 + r)$$

Subtracting Equation (5.3) from Equation (5.4), we get

$$FVA[(1 + r)^{n} - 1]/r = A = PVIFA(r,n)\dots..(5.5)$$

Therefore, $PVIFA(r,n) = FVIFAIr,n) + PVIF(i,n)$

The $FVIFA_{(r,n)}$ values for different combinations of *r* and *n* are given in Appendix 1

Annuity due

In the case of annuity, it is generally assumed that a payment has been made at the end of each year. If payment is made at the beginning of each year, then this is called annuity due, and its value is found by the product of the value either present or future of a regular annuity and the factor $(1 + r)$.

$$FVA_{n}(due) = A + FVIFA_{(r,n)} = (1 + r)$$

$$PVA_{n}(due) = A + PVIFA_{(r,n)} + (1 + r)$$

125

For instance, the present value of a 5-year annuity due of $ 5,000 at 10% will be:

$PVA_n(due) = A + PVIFA_{(i,n)} + (1 + i) = \$ 5,000 + PVIFA_{(10.5)} + (1 + 0.10) = \$ 20,850.5$.

Perpetuity

Frequently, an investment pays a fixed sum each year for a specified number of years. A series of annual receipts or payments is termed an annuity. The imprest form of an annuity for an infinite series is called perpetuity.

For example, government stocks contain a fixed annual income, but there is no obligation to repay the capital. The present value of such stocks (called irredeemable) is found by dividing the annual sum received by the annual rate of interest.

$PV_{perpetuity} = A/r$

Or, $(1 + r)^n = FV/PV$

$r = (FV/PV)V_n - 1$

For instance, if a credit company offers to lend you $ 1,000 today on a condition that you repay $ 1,643 at the end of 3 years, then the compound interest rate for this would be:
$i = (1,643/1,000)1/3 - 1 = 1.8\%$

5.7 Cost of Capital

Each agribusiness firm has to spend a certain amount of money either to generate capital from the market or to hold capital within it. This is known as the cost of capital.

The cost of capital concept has a very important role to play within agribusiness finance. It is the company's cost of capital that is used as the discount rate in the investment appraisal process. We assume that an agribusiness firm is a rational agent and so it will seek to raise capital by the cheapest and most efficient methods, hence minimizing its cost of capital. It first requires information on costs associated with the different ways of raising finance. Second, it needs to know how to combine the different sources of finance in order to reach its optimal capital structure.

The cost of source of finance is defined as the rate of discount that equates the present value of the expected payments of a source of finance with the net proceeds received from the same source.

5.7.1 Opportunity cost of capital

A firm can have different sources of funding and each consumes different costs. Therefore, if a firm selects a particular type of capital and foregoes the other, the income foregone is known as the opportunity cost of capital.

The first step in calculating a company's weighted average cost of capital (WACC) is to calculate the cost of the individual components of its capital. Here, we consider the different sources of long-term finance available to a company and how to calculate the cost of using the source.

5.7.2 Cost of equity

Though equity is the owner's capital, a significant amount is required to generate equity capital and to hold it over a period of time by way of cost of issuing equity, administrative cost, agency cost, dividend distribution cost, and other related costs. These costs collectively constitute the cost of equity.

Equity finance can be raised either through issuing new securities or through the utilization of retained earnings. To find out the cost of equity (k), we can adapt the Gordon growth model for the valuation of equity capital as follows:

According to the dividend forecast approach, the intrinsic value of an equity to the sum of the present values of the dividends associated with it, is given as:

$$P_i = Di/(1 + k_n)/I \text{ for } i = \text{to } n$$

Where,
P_i = price per equity share,
Di = expected dividend per share at the end of year,
K_i = rate of return required by the equity shareholders,

The cost of equity, from the firm's point of view, is the rate at which the intrinsic value of the market price of the share is equal to the discounted value of the dividends. Assuming the constant growth rate in dividends, the above equation can be written as:

$$P_i = D_i / (k_i = g)$$

$$P_{r \cdot K_i} = (Di/Pi) + g = (D_n(1 + g) / P_n) + g$$

where P_n = ex-dividend current share price,

g = expected annual in dividends,

D_n = dividend to be paid shortly,

D_1 = dividend to be paid after one year.

5.8 Steps in Investment Analysis

The following steps are involved in applying the net present value method for analysing agribusiness capital investment.

- *Identify the investment to be analyzed* (e.g. tractor, combine harvester, milk delivery truck, dairy cows, land reclamation etc.) after making a thorough search for all investment possibilities. It is important not to limit the analysis to only one possibility; consider other alternatives that may be better investments.
- *Determine the initial cash outlay required* to make the investment. This is the total amount of cash required, whether borrowed or not.
- *Estimate the annual net cash flows* that result from the investment for each year of the planning period. These annual cash flows include only those changes in receipts or expenses resulting directly from a farm investment. Do not include those that would occur regardless of the investment. Include the salvage value of the investment, if any, as a positive cash flow in the last year.
- *Choose the discount rate.* The discount, or interest, rate is the investor's minimum acceptable rate of return, and should reflect the interest paid on the debt and the opportunity cost of the equity invested. The opportunity cost is that rate of return the

investor would expect to earn if the money were invested in the best alternative.

- *Calculate the net present values* of the cash outlay to purchase the investment and the annual net cash flows resulting from the investment by multiplying the amount for each year by the appropriate discount factor and then summing the discounted amounts. The result is the net present value of the investment.

- *Decide whether to accept the investment.* If the net present value is positive, then the returns to the proposed investment will more than cover the cost of capital; and the investment is profitable. If the net present value is negative, it is not a viable investment.

5.9 Decision Making Tools for Investment Analysis

There is a large choice of measures of project worth which can be grouped into two types: non-discounted and discounted.

5.9.1 Non-discounted measures of project worth

The first group - the non-discounted measures - use the cash flow as obtained through the project period without taking the present value of future flows into consideration. The most used non-discounted measures of project worth are: ranking by inspection, payback period and return on investment.

5.9.1.1 Ranking by inspection

A project analyst should ask the following question: Given alternative investments, which one should be implemented and which one should be discarded? This question is important since we can have a situation of mutually exclusive investments. In such circumstances, it is technically impossible to undertake these projects.

In this case, ranking by inspection of investments can be used. Ranking by Inspection consists of choosing the best investment by comparing the net proceeds of alternative investments. The project having more cash proceeds will be preferred. But there are some peculiarities in ranking investments by inspection as is shown in the example in Table 5.9

Suppose a project analyst is presented alternative investments out of which he must select one as a first choice for implementation. After comparing the net cash proceeds of two projects, A and B, we can find out which project has the shorter life period.

Then we compare the proceeds of the short-lived project with the long-lived one. If the two projects have the same initial investment and the same proceeds throughout the period of the short-lived investment, and if the long-lived investment continues to earn income after the end of the short-lived one, then, the long-lived one is more desirable; because all things being equal, the second project continues to earn proceeds while the first one has ended.

This is the case for Investment A and B having an identical investment outlay, and the same proceeds of $20,000 during the life period of A, but Investment B continues to earn $2,000 after A has been terminated. Investment B is therefore more desirable than A.

Let us now look at project C and D (Table 5.9).They has an identical initial investment outlay. In addition, they have the same life period of two years, and the net proceeds throughout the life period is identical. Which one, C or D, is more desirable?

Table 5.10: Net Cash Flow of Four Hypothetical Project Alternatives ($)

Project Investment	Initial Cost	Net Cash Proceeds		
		Year 1	Year 2	Total
A	20,000	20,000	–	20,000
B	20,000	20,000	2,000	22,000
C	20,000	14,625	9,825	24,450
D	20,000	16,325	8,125	24,450

In this special case, although the total net proceeds is identical ($24,450), the project that earns more income early than the other is more desirable. In the example, after year 1, Investment C has produced a net cash flow of $14,625 while Investment D has obtained $16,325 or an additional $1,700. This $1,700 would be earned by Investment C only in year 2. Investment D is more desirable because it earns $1,700 *earlier* than Investment C.

5.9.1.2 Payback period

The question answered by the payback period is: How long will it take to earn an amount of proceeds equal to the initial cost of investment? The answer to this question involves the calculation of the length of the period that is required for the stream of the earned cash proceeds to equal the initial cost of investment.

If the net annual proceeds are constant, the payback period in years is found by dividing the total initial outlay by the amount of expected annual cash proceeds. For instance, if the total initial cost of investment is $500, and if the net amount proceeds is $100, for 10 years, the payback period would be $500 divided by 100, or five years. If the annual proceeds are not constant, the payback period will be obtained by finding out after how many years the total net proceeds will equal the original outlay. This is done by adding up the net proceeds year to year, until the amount of the initial investment cost is reached. An example of calculation of the payback period on the basis of the previous table is shown in Table 5.10.

Table 5.11: Payback Period

Investment	Payback period (Year)	Ranking
A	1	1
B	1	1
C	1.5	4
D	1.4	3

Although Investments A and B have the same payback period, Investment B is preferable, because it earns more proceeds than Investment A. Investment B earns $2,000 above the $20,000 also earned by Investment A.

Considering Investments C and D, both have identical payback periods of two years. But looking at the proceeds earned, Investment D will have earned $1,700 more than Investment C only in the first year. Therefore, although Investments C and D have the same payback period, Investment D is preferable because it earns more than Investment C in the earlier period.

Thus, the payback period measure has two deficiencies:

- It fails to take the proceeds earned after the payback period into account; and
- It does not account for the timing of proceeds earned prior to the payback period date.

For these two reasons, some project analysts disqualify this measure of project selection. But there is at least one more measure, namely the concept of return on investment.

5.9.1.3 Return on Investment

This measure is also called average income on cost. It should be clearly differentiated with the internal rate of return, which is a discounted measure. Average income on cost is formed by dividing the average income by the cost of investment as is shown in Table 5.11.

Table 5.12: Average Income on Cost

Investment	Cost ($)	Average Income($)	Average Income on Cost (%)	Ranking
A	20,000	0	0	4
B	20,000	660	3.3	3
C	20,000	800	4	1
D	20,000	800	4	1

Some private investors use a similar ratio whereby the average income is divided by the book value. In second alternative the average income is computed after depreciation. In this context, projects C and D are preferred because they have higher average income.

5.9.2 Discounted Measures of Project Worth

The non-discounted measures of project worth have one serious shortfall: they do not take into account the difference between the value of money today, and the same value in the future. By contrast, the discounted measures of project worth - Net Present Value, Cost-

Benefit Analysis, and Internal Rate of Return - are based on the concept that "to receive some today is better than to receive more tomorrow." The discounted measures of project worth of an investment use the present value of future costs and returns. While two of these measures have been discussed previously, they are reviewed again here to highlight their importance in project assessment.

- Three important measures of project worth incorporating the principles of discounting are:
  - ❏ Net Present Value (NPV)
  - ❏ Internal Rate of Return (IRR)
  - ❏ Benefit-Cost Ratio (B/C)

5.9.2.1 Net Present value (NPV)

The net present value (NPV) of an investment is the present (discounted) value of future cash inflows minus the present value of the investment and any associated future cash outflows. Essentially, It is the net result of a multiyear investment expressed in today's shillings. By considering the time value of money, it allows consideration of such things as cost of capital, interest rates and investment opportunity costs. It is especially appropriate for long-term projects. Ranking investments by NPV does not compare absolute levels of investment. NPV looks at cash flows, not at profits and losses the way accounting systems do. NPV is highly sensitive to the discount percentage, and that can be tricky to determine. Projects with a positive NPV are expected to increase the value of the firm. Thus, the NPV decision rule specifies that all independent projects with a positive NPV should be accepted. When choosing among mutually exclusive projects, the project with the largest (positive) NPV should be selected.

The NPV is calculated as the present value of the project's cash inflows minus the present value of the project's cash outflows. This relationship is expressed by the following formula:

$$NPV = \sum_{t=0}^{T} \frac{CF_t}{(1+r)^t} = CF_0 + \frac{CF_1}{(1+r)^1} + \frac{CF_2}{(1+r)^2} + ... + \frac{CF_T}{(1+r)^T}$$

- Where

CF_t = the cash flow at time t and CF_t= b-c

r = the cost of capital (interest rate).

$$NPV = \frac{b_n - c_n}{(1+r)^n}$$

Annuity formula

With salvage value:

$$NPV = \sum_{r=1}^{n} \frac{CF}{(1+r)^n} + \frac{Rn}{(1+r)^n} = A \text{ (investment)}$$

$$PV_n = A \left[\frac{(1+r^n)-1}{r(1+r)^n} \right]$$

The example in Table 5.12 illustrates calculation of Net Present Value. Consider projects A and B, which yield the following cash flows over their five-year lives. The cost of capital for the project is 10%.

Table 5.13: Net Present Value Calculations

Year	Project A Cash Flow	Project B Cash Flow
0	$– 1000	$– 1000
1	500	100
2	400	200
3	200	200
4	200	400
5	100	700

Net Present Value
Project A:

$$NPV = -1000 + \frac{500}{(1=10)^1} + \frac{400}{(1+10)^2} + \frac{200}{(1+10)^3} + \frac{200}{(1+10)^4} + \frac{100}{(1+10)^5} = TShs.134.08$$

Project B:

$$NPV = -1000 + \frac{100}{(1=10)^1} + \frac{200}{(1+10)^2} + \frac{200}{(1+10)^3} + \frac{400}{(1+10)^4} + \frac{700}{(1+10)^5} = TShs.114.31$$

Thus, if Projects A and B are independent projects then both projects should be accepted. On the other hand, if they are mutually exclusive projects then Project A should be chosen since it has the larger NPV.NPV considers the time value of money. In this example (Table 5.13), we compare two $ 1 million projects with a minimum desired rate of return of 10%. On the basis of simple cash flow, the ATM installation looks better because it generates $250,000 more over the life of the investment. But when the time value of money is considered, the server consolidation project looks slightly better, with an NPV higher by $9,000, because the returns occur earlier in the project's life.

Table 5.14: Net Present Value

Year	Discount factor (at 10%)	ATM installation		Server consolidation
		Cash flow	Present value if cash flow	Cash flow
0	1.000	-$1 million	-$1 million	-$ million
1	0.909	+$500,000	+$454,500	+$1million
2	0.826	+500,000	+$413,500	+$750,000
3	0.751	+500,000	+$375,500	+$500,000
4	0.683	+$500,000	+$341,500	
5	0.621	+$500,000	+$310,500	
Total	+$1.5 million	+895,000	+$1.25 million	+$904,000

5.9.2.2 Internal Rate of Return

The internal rate of return (IRR) is the discount rate that results in a net present value of zero for a series of cash flows. Essentially, it's a cut-off rate of return. Avoid an investment or project if its IRR is less than the cost of capital or minimum desired rate of return. It provides a simple hurdle rate for investment decision-making and is the method favoured by many accountants and finance people. The IRR concept is not as easy to understand as some measures and not as easy to compute (even Excel uses approximations). Computational anomalies can produce misleading results, particularly with regard to reinvestments. The determination of the IRR for a project, generally, involves trial and error or a numerical technique (see below). Fortunately, financial calculators greatly simplify this process. The IRR decision rule specifies that all independent projects with an IRR greater than the cost of capital should be accepted. When choosing among mutually exclusive projects, the project with the highest IRR should be selected (as long as the IRR is greater than the cost of capital).

$$NPV=0 \sum_{t=0}^{T} \frac{CF_t}{(1=IRR)^t} = CF_0 + \frac{CF_1}{(1+IRR)^2} + \frac{CF_2}{(1=IRR)} + ... + \frac{CF_T}{(1+IRR)}$$

where

CFt = the cash flow at time t and IRR is the Internal Rate of Return.

The example in Table 5.14 and 5.15 illustrates the determination of IRR. Consider projects A and B, which yield the following cash flows over their five-year lives. The cost of capital for both projects is 10%.

Table 5.15: Determination of Internal Rate of Return

Year	Cash Flow	Cash Flow
0	$-1000	$- 1000
1	500	100
2	400	200
3	200	200
4	200	400
5	100	700

Project A:

$$0=-1000+\frac{500}{(1+IRR)^1}+\frac{400}{(1+IRR)^2}+\frac{200}{(1+IRR)^3}+\frac{200}{(1+IRR)^4}+\frac{100}{(1+IRR)^5}$$

$\therefore IRR=16.82\%$

Project B:

$$0=-1000+\frac{100}{(1+IRR)^1}+\frac{200}{(1+IRR)^2}+\frac{200}{(1+IRR)^3}+\frac{200}{(1+IRR)^4}+\frac{700}{(1+IRR)^5}$$

$\therefore IRR=13.28\%$

Thus, if Projects A and B are independent projects then both projects should be accepted since their IRRs are greater than the cost of capital. On the other hand, if they are mutually exclusive projects then Project A should be chosen since it has the higher IRR.

Table 5.16: Internal Rate of ReturnDetermination

Year	Cash flow	Discount rate 10%		Discount rate: 15%		Discount rate: 20%	
		Factor	Amount	Factor	Amount	Factor	Amount
0	-$1 million	1.000	$1million	1.000	-0$1 million	1.000	-$ million
1	+$300,000	0.909	$273,000	0.870	$261,000	0.833	$250,000
2	+$300,000	0.826	$248,000	0.756	$227,000	0.694	$208,000
3	+$300,000	0.751	$225,000	0.658	$197,000	0.579	$174,000
4	+$300,000	0.683	$205,000	0.572	$172,000	0.482	$145,000
5	+$300,000	0.621	$186,000	0.497	$149,000	0.402	$121,000
Total	+$500,000	NPV =	$137,000	NPV=+$6,000	+6,000	NPV=$102,000	NPV=$102,000
		IRR = slightly more than 15%					

Exact calculation of the IRR requires some computation. For that reason, an approximation is often favoured. The approximation procedure is based on the principle that an interpolation between a positive and a negative net present value approximately comes close to the condition of a net present value of zero.

Steps in approximating the IRR:

❏ Choose two different discount rates, one leading to a positive NPV, the other to a negative NPV.

❏ Interpolate between these two NPVs using the formula:

$$IRR = r_1 + \frac{(r_n - r_1) \times NPV(r_1)}{\left| NPV(r_1) \right| + \left| NPV(r_n) \right|}$$

where:

r_1 lower discount rate

r_h higher discount rate

For simple accept/reject decisions, both give the same message:

❑   If NPV > 0, accept.

❑   If IRR > cost of capital, accept.

Since any agribusiness financial analysis must calculate cash flows for NPV, estimating IRR should be done concurrently. Problems may occur when choosing *between* investments if they are mutually exclusive. NPV is superior to IRR in ranking exclusive investments or limited capital

5.9.2.3 Benefit Cost Ratio: The BCR is the ratio of all the discounted (yearly) incremental benefits and costs of a project. Thus, it expresses the benefit generated by the project per unit of cost of the project expressed in present values and is calculated as follows:

$$BCR = \frac{\sum_{t=1}^{n} \frac{B_t}{(1 = r)^t}}{\sum_{t=1}^{n} \frac{(C_t)}{(1 + r)^t}} \text{ where,}$$

$B_t =$ incremental benefit in period t,

$C_t =$ incremental cost in period t,

r= discount rate in %,

n =years of project duration.

The BCR expresses the benefit generated per unit of cost and is interpreted as follows:

❑ BCR > 1: present value of benefits exceeds the present value of costs.

❑ BCR = 1: present value of benefits equals present value of costs.

❑ BCR < 1: the present value of costs exceeds the present value of benefits.

To select which project is most viable, use the following selection criteria. Projects with a BCR of 1 or greater are economically acceptable when the costs and benefit streams are discounted at the opportunity cost of capital. The absolute value of the BCR varies depending on the discount rate chosen; the higher the discount rate, the smaller the BCR.

Table 5.17: Benefit Cost Ratio

T	Incremental Benefits			Incremental costs		
	Benefits	Discount factor 5%	Present worth	Costs	Discount factor 5%	Present worth
1	0	0.952381	0	1100	0.952381	1047.619
2	400	0.907029	362.8118	150	0.907029	136.0544
3	400	0.863838	345.5350	150	0.863838	129.5756
4	400	0.822702	329.0810	150	0.822702	123.4054
5	400	0.783526	313.4105	150	0.783526	117.5289
6	400	0.746215	298.4862	150	0.746215	111.9323
7	400	0.710681	284.2725	150	0.710681	106.6022
Total	2400		1933.6	2000		1772.7

5.10 Comparing Discounted and Non-Discounted Measures of Worthiness

Each of the discounted and non-discounted measures of project worthiness has its strengths and weaknesses. Table 5.17 gives a comparative assessment of the discounted and non-discounted measures of worthiness in terms of a number of selected variables shown in column 1. Further discussion of merits and demerits of specific measures are given in subsequent sections after the table.

Table 5.18: Comparison of Discounted Measures of Project Worth

Item	Net Present Value (NPV)	Internal Rate of Return (IRR)
Selection criterion	Accept all independent projects with NPV of zero or greater when discounted at opportunity cost of capital	Accept all independent projects with IRR equal to or greater than opportunity cost of capital.
Ranking	Gives ranking for order of implementation, if investment costs are equal.	May give incorrect ranking among independent project.
Mutually exclusive alternatives	Accept alternative with largest NPV when discounted at opportunity cost of capital. (NPV is the preferred selection criterion for mutually exclusive alternatives).	Cannot be used directly; must discount differences between incremental net benefit flows of mutually exclusive alternative projects.
Discount rate	Must determine a suitable discount rate, generally the opportunity cost of capital.	Determined internally; must determine opportunity cost of capital to use as a cut-off rate.
Advantages	Takes into account time value of money. It takes into account scale of investment	It provides a measure of the rate of return on capital invested. No decision is required for appropriate discount. More easy understood than NPV.
Disadvantage	It take no account of capital required. It is not always easy for untrained people to understand. It requires decision on the appropriate discount rate.	It takes no account of scale of investment. It take no account of timing of cash flow. Cannot be calculated when all costs positive.

Net Present Value

Advantages:
- It takes account of time preference for money
- It takes account of scale of investment. IRR will normally be the same.

Disadvantages
- It takes no account of capital required. IRR can enable ranking as it will be higher for low capital investment and vice versa.
- It is not always easy for untrained people to understand.
- It requires a decision on the appropriate discount rate.

Internal Rate of Return (from financier's point of view)
Advantages:
- It provides a measure of the rate of return on capital invested
- No decision is required as to the appropriate discount rate.
- It is thought to be more easily understood than NPV

Disadvantages:
It needs to be admitted that IRR suffers from some inherent computational problems, which goes against its acceptability under certain circumstances. In addition to the above drawback, its greatest demerit lies in the concept of reinvestment rate assumption, which is an implicit factor in IRR computation visa vis decisions applying IRR method.

Example: The life of both projects A and B is two years and the appropriate rate of discount for both projects can be taken as 10%. Other information, i.e., initial investment, cash inflows, NPV, and IRR are given in table 5.18.

Table 5.19: Conflict between NPV and IRR

Project	Initial Investment ($)	Cash inflow ($)		NPV	IRR
		Year X	Year Y		
A	100	200	0	81.82	100%
B	100	0	400	230.50	100%

As per NPV, B is better, and as per IRR, both projects have equal weightage. Other disadvantages are:

- ❏ It takes no account of scale of investment.
- ❏ It takes not account of timing of cash flows.
- ❏ It cannot be calculated when all cash flows are positive or all negative. This is a theoretical limitation.
- ❏ Negative cash flows at the end of the investment's life may cause problems of multiple yields or overstate the true IRR.

CHAPTER SIX

Managing Risks and Uncertainties in Agribusiness Projects

6.1 Introduction

In any project evaluation there is a great deal of uncertainty. For example, the analyst may be uncertain of benefits, costs, shadow prices, the social discount rate or a combination of these variables. The problem is to test the project in order to show the effect of any assumptions and possible related uncertainties on the result of the assessment. This analysis is known as sensitivity analysis. Its aim is to determine which of the assumptions concerning the project should be subjected to further study. It is a simple technique in which different values are attached to uncertain variables in order to demonstrate to the decision-maker what the effect of variations in the assumptions will be.

It is an attempt to show how sensitive the decision is to certain assumptions. With the aid of a sensitivity analysis the marginality of a project can be determined, i.e. how sensitive the funding criteria are in respect of the assumptions and how sensitive the ranking of projects is in respect of the assumptions.

Sensitivity analysis must not, however, be misused in presentation. It must not serve as an excuse for not quantifying and must not be presented as a complicated set of conversion rules which cannot identify a clear first choice for the decision-maker. If carried out properly, sensitivity analysis will lead to more optimal decisions, and it should go without saying that such an analysis will accompany the results of a cost-benefit analysis.

6.2 The Concept of Risk and Uncertainty

In a discussion of investment criteria, it is generally assumed that the costs and benefits of an investment are known with certainty. This is not normally the case, as these costs and benefits lie in an uncertain future. Project appraisal is future-oriented planning and therefore based on estimations of future costs, benefits, demand, prices etc. So far we

143

looked at deterministic decision models (with complete information). The future being uncertain poses a lot of questions as to whether the information is likely to occur, wither or undergo any varying degree of change. Whatever the expectation, it is necessary to ascertain the extent to which results are likely to occur, and draw a strategy regarding what should be done to ameliorate unforeseen circumstances. In project planning and management, sensitivity analysis performs this function. The amount of uncertainty about our estimates is likely to vary from one investment to another and this uncertainty is something to be taken into account in making decisions on which investment to carry out.

6.2.1 Non-discounted measures (short-cuts) in dealing with uncertainty

(i) Payback period

- To avoid problems associated with future uncertainties, projects are selected on merits, depending on the period within which the initial capital investment is recouped.
- At times the period of re-crumpet is a subject of policy, so much so that it is a priori determined.
- In such circumstances, it is the project that recoups the initial investment costs within a short period. The idea behind this is that the sooner the initial capital is recovered, the more secure investors will be with the project (see example Table 6.1).

Table 6.1: Cash flows to Establish the Payback Period

Projects	Year 1	Year 2	Year 3	Year 4	Year 5	Year 6	Year 7
Project A	-100	20	20	25	30	50	75
Project B	-100	30	45	60	15	-	-
Project C	-100	60	45	30	15		5

- Project A recoups the initial capital investment after six years including the year of investment.

- Project B recoups the initial capital investment after four years.

- Project C recoups the initial capital investment after three years and is selected as it recoups the initial capital investment quicker.

(iii)   Changing the value of project streams

The above technique is not without inherent drawbacks, especially with regard to uncertainty. One way to mitigate this is to increase project costs by a given percentage - in this case 10%. Alternatively, the same percentage can be used to decrease the value of project benefits. The choice of percent increase or decrease usually depends on the rate of inflation or expected rate of price increase. The aim is to find out whether costs or benefits decrease by that proportion, in which case the project would still be worth implementing (Table 6.2 – 6.4).

Table 6.2: Unadjusted Project Stream of Benefits and Costs ($ 00,00)

Project	0	1	2	3	4	5	6	7
PV Benefits	0	13	8.2	10	11	11	11	11
PV Costs	15	0.9	7.4	9	10.1	10.1	10.1	10.1
Net Benefits	-15	12.1	0.8	1	0.9	0.9	0.9	0.9

NPV = $ 252,000

Table 6.3: Increase in Cost by 10% ($00,000)

Project	0	1	2	3	4	5	6	7
PV Costs	15	0.9	7.4	9	10.1	10.1	10.1	10.1
10% Increase	1.5	1.5	0.09	0.74	0.9	1.01	1.01	
PV Costs (adj.)	16.5	0.99	8.14	9.9	11.11	11.11	11.11	11.11

Table 6.4: Adjusted Stream of Benefits and Costs(Ths.00,000)

Project	0	1	2	3	4	5	6	7
PV Benefit	-	13.00	8.20	10.00	11.00	11.00	11.00	11.00
PV Costs	16.5	0.99	8.14	9.9	11.11	11.11	11.11	11.11
Net Benefit	16.5	12.01	0.06	0.1	-0.11	-0.11	-0.11	-0.11

NPV = $ 474,000

The example above shows that the project was acceptable with a NPV of $ 252,000. However, the increase of costs by only 10% reduced the NPV of the same project by $s. 726,000, i.e. from $ 252,000 to $

474,000. This shows the unstable nature of the project net benefits to increase in project costs.

(iii) Use of contingency

In some cases a contingency element is introduced in project planning. Depending on the nature of uncertainty, the investment, operating or total costs may be increased by some percentage. In the final analysis, the changes will have increased the costs of undertaking the project.

If a project passes the test, it is accepted for implementation as being less sensitive to increased costs. If it does not, the project is rejected on the grounds that it is uncertain.

(iv)   Use of risk adjusted discount rate

In some cases the uncertainty surrounding the project is tested using a certain percentage increase in the discount rate. The discount rate initially used has to reflect the commercial or economic conditions facing the project in question. This may be the borrowing or lending rate, depending on the opportunity cost. Given the rated uncertainty, a discount rate is increased by a given percentage say, 2%. The increase in the discount rate reduces the future value more than it was the case.

Table 6.5: Discount factors 10% for 7 years

Project	0	1	2	3	4	5	6	7
Discount factor	1.00	0.909	0.826	0.683	0.621	0.621	0.564	0.513
Factor by 10%	1.000	8.893	0.797	0.712	0.636	0567	0.507	0.452

Table 6.5 shows that the new discount factor penalizes the net benefits much more, and thus results in much smaller values. This is more likely to reduce the attractiveness of the envisaged project. It is very much possible for the result obtained to render the project unacceptable. If such changes leave the decision on the project unchanged, then it is convincing that the project can be implemented without concern for its returns.

6.3 Safety Margins and Switching Values

Most of the techniques used in dealing with uncertainty assume that the uncertainty facing the project is global, such that one is compelled to accept or reject a project, depending on the results obtained. Such situations are rare and somehow unrealistic. In practice one is likely to be faced with a single project and possibly with several alternative versions (the latter is a mutually exclusive project situation). The former is then of a primary concern in this case.

Logically it is useful to consider a project as comprising several components. It is equally logical, when one considers the degree of uncertainty facing project components that differ from each other and that of facing the project as a whole. It is because of this reality that sensitivity analysis has to perform tests to identify those sensitive variables to which the project is dependent upon. It is not very likely that the several project components will be systematically tested to ascertain project sensitivity. The variables chosen for analysis will very much depend on the knowledge about the project's components and environment under which the project will be implemented. More often, but not mandatory, one needs to carry out tests on major variables in the project.

Variations in such major items are likely to bring changes in values obtained at the analysis stage. Examples of such variables are investment costs, price or, major inputs, selling price of outputs, and variations on the cost of capital. The methodology used to carry out sensitivity analysis involves the calculation of two values: safety margins and switching values. Though they differ, they tend to complement each other and lead to the same decision.

6.3.1 Safety Margins

The **safety margin** of a variable is a percent change in the variable that reduces the net present value (NPV) of a project to zero, essentially providing a given variable with space to allow for some degree of flexibility. The smaller the percentage the variable has to be changed before the net present value (of a project turns to zero), the more sensitive the variable. The reverse is true, if such a percentage is high.

Safety margin = (% change in variable/% change in NPV) * 100

6.3.2 *Switching values*

The switching value, on the other hand, addresses the same issue but from a different perspective. The **switching value** seeks to establish the value of the variable, which turns the net present value of the project to zero.

Switching value = Original value – (Original value x Safety margin)

For the purpose of demonstration, only three components will be tested. These are:

- ❑   Investment costs;
- ❑   Operating costs; and
- ❑   Selling price of outputs.

Example: Increase in investment costs

Errors committed while estimating investment costs are often responsible for stalled projects. To be certain about the behaviour of such variable, we investigate the effects on the net present value of increasing investment costs by 15% at 12% rate of discount (Table 6.6) as shown in the following example.

By these results, it seems that the project is less sensitive to an increase in investment costs. In order for the NPV of the project to be reduced to zero, the investment costs have to increase by 300%. One explanation for the insensitive results could be that investment costs are only a small proportion of the costs in this project.

Table 6.6: Sensitivity Analysis

Year	Investment Cost	15% Increase	Discount factor 12%	Change in NPV (12%)
0	39.6	5.94	1.00	5.94
1			0.893	
2			0.797	
3			0.712	
4			0.636	
5	1.0	0.15	0.567	0.085
6			0.507	
7			0.452	
8			0.404	
9			0.361	
10			0.33	0.048
11			0.287	
12			0.257	
13			0.229	
14			0.205	
15			0.183	
16	-8.7	-1.31	0.163	-0.213
Total				5.861

The original NPV is $ 11,870,000.
Percentage change in NPV = (586,100 ÷ 11,870,000) x 100
Percentage change in NPV = 5%
Safety margin = (0.15 ÷ 0.05) = x100
Safety margin = 300%

Example: Increase in operating costs

In this case we wish to examine the effect on the NPV of the increase in operating costs by 15% at a 12% discount rate. The original NPV is $ 11,870,000.

Table 6.7: Increase in operating cost by 15% and the effect on NPV ($ 00,000)

Year	Operating Cost	15% Increase	Discount factor 12%	Change NPV (12%)
0	0	0.000	1.000	0.000
1	325.3	48.795	0.893	43.567
2	388.9	64.68	0.797	46.504
3	431.2	64.68	0.712	46.038
4	431.2	64.68	0.636	41.105
5	431.2	64.68	0.576	36.701
6	431.2	64.68	0.507	32.769
7	431.2	64.68	0.452	29.258
8	431.2	64.68	0.404	26.123
9	431.2	64.68	0.361	23.324
10	431.2	64.68	0.322	20.825
11	431.2	64.68	0.287	18.594
12	431.2	64.68	0.257	16.602
13	431.2	64.68	0.229	14.823
14	431.2	64.68	0.205	13.235
15	431.2	64.68	0.183	11.817
16	431.2	64.68	0.163	10.551
Total				431.836

The 15% increase in operating costs decreases the NPV of the project at 12% rate of discount by 431.836%. To decrease the NPV of the project to zero, the operating costs would have to increase only by about 4.1%, i.e. this margin is very sensitive to an increase in operating costs. Without going into detailed computations, this kind of the project requires that the management should strive to maintain the operating costs at the current levels due to the fact that this variable is very critical.

Any increase of the same is likely to jeopardize the acceptability of the project. If it turns out that the management or project owners are not in a position of doing this, it may be wise to reject the project irrespective of the initially attractive NPV of $ 11,870,000.

Example: Decrease in selling price of output

In this case we wish to investigate the effect on NPV at 12% of a 15% decrease in output price. This is likely to occur due to number of reasons, including competition, availability of substitutes, etc.

Table 6.8: Effect of 15% decrease in output price on NPV ($00,000)

Year	Price/ tonne	15% Decrease	Output (t)	Value decrease	DF 12%	Change in NPV (12%)
0	0	0.0	0.0	0.0	1.000	0.00
1	3700	555	7.5	4162.5	0.893	3716.52
2	3700	555	9.0	4995.0	0.797	3981.98
3	3700	555	10.0	5550.0	0.712	3950.38
4	3700	555	10.0	5550.0	0.636	3527.13
5	3700	555	10.0	5550.0	0.567	3149.22
6	3700	555	10.0	5550.0	0.507	2811.80
7	3700	555	10.0	5550.0	0.452	2510.54
8	3700	555	10.0	5550.0	0.404	2241.55
9	3700	555	10.0	5550.0	0.361	2001.39
10	3700	555	10.0	5550.0	0.322	1786.95
11	3700	555	10.0	5550.0	0.287	1595.49
12	3700	555	10.0	5550.0	0.257	1424.55
13	3700	555	10.0	5550.0	0.229	1271.92
14	3700	555	10.0	5550.0	0.205	1135.64
15	3700	555	10.0	5550.0	0.183	1013.96
16	3700	555	10.0	5550.0	0.163	905.33
Total						37024.34

The original NPV is $ 11,870,000.
Percentage change in NPV =   (37,024.34 ÷ 11,870,000) x 100
Percentage change in NPV =   311.9%
Safety margin =   4.81%

Switching value = original value – (Original value x safety margin)
Switching value =   3700 – (3700 x 0.0481)
Switching value =   3522

A 15% decrease in the selling price of cotton lint reduces the NPV of the project at 12% from $ 11,870,000 to $ –37,024,340. To reduce NPV

151

to zero, the price needs only to fall by 4.81%; that is in order to break even, the output (cotton lint price will have to be $ 3,522). This variable is equally sensitive and thus serious attention should be paid.

Major advantages of sensitivity analysis

Sensitivity analysis allows decision makers to be more informed about project sensitivities, or in other words, allows them to know the room they have for judgmental errors. Thus, they can decide whether they are in a position to accept risk. If sensitivity analysis points to some variables as more crucial than others, then the search time and the money can be concentrated with the objective of controlling and laying special emphasis on these variables. During the implementation phase of the investment process, sensitivity analysis may be used to highlight these factors, which makes a greater impact on NPV. Then these factors may be monitored more carefully in order to control major deviation from their project values.

Major drawbacks of sensitivity analysis

The absence of any formal assignment of probabilities to the variation of crucial parameters is a potential limitation of sensitivity analysis. The concept may be best understood in relation to the case under review. For example, the discount rate may change considerably before break even NPV is reached, whereas the price can only change slightly. Thus, at the first glance one may conclude that NPV is more vulnerable to the price change than to the variability of the discount rate. However, if the prices are controlled by government regulations, there is a very low probability of the price changing; whereas if the probability of changing the discount rate is very high, a re-assessment of the relative risk may be in order. Thus, this is an example where mathematical formulation can be a poor substitute for judgment.

CHAPTER SEVEN

Implementing the Project

7.1 Introduction

The implementation stage of project management is the most important since all plans highlighted in previous phases are put into reality. In this chapter three important dimensions of project implementation are discussed. These are financial management, procurement and management of materials, and management of human resources.

7.2 Objectives of Project Implementation

Project implementation is usually guided by pre-determined objectives, which can be grouped under three types:

Performance and quality

The end result of the project must be fit for the purpose for which it was intended. The project owner and all the other stakeholders must be satisfied (refer chapter 2 & 3). Most work on project management, e.g. achievement of time and cost objectives, quality assurance, and performance and reliability, obviously requires competence in design. The design must consider the following:

Budget (cost)

The project must be completed without exceeding the authorized expenditure. For commercial and industrial agribusiness projects, failure to complete work within the authorized budget will reduce profits and the expected return on the capital invested, with risks of a loss or a more serious (and terminal) financial outcome.

Time to completion

Actual progress has to match or exceed planned progress. All significant stages of the project must take place no later than their specified dates to result in total completion on or before the planned finish date. Late completion or delivery of agribusiness projects, to say the least, will not please the project clients or sponsors. A common risk to agribusiness projects is failure to start work on time. Very long delays can be caused by procrastination, delays in supply deliveries, legal or planning difficulties, shortage of information, lack of funds or other resources, and a host of other reasons. All of these factors can place a farm manager in a difficult or impossible position. Delays during the project establishment timeline inevitably result in late start dates and potentially lost revenue.

The overall objective is to complete the project within the time, cost and quality premium set. To achieve this the agribusiness project manager must subdivide the project's scope of work into a list of project activities with associated objectives. The objectives associated with these activities can now be clearly identified and communicated to the responsible parties. The use of graphics (bar-charts, networks) will greatly assist the dissemination process.

The triangle of forces is often used to graphically outline the trade-off between the main parameters of time, cost and quality.

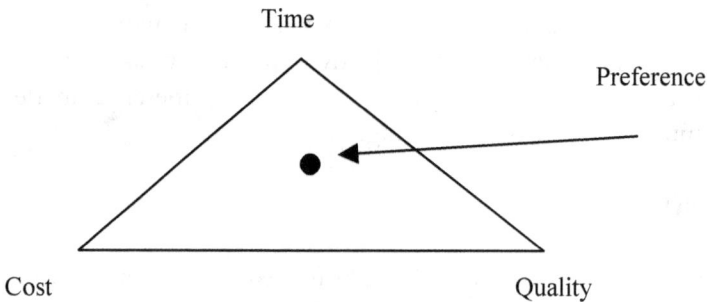

Time

Preference

Cost   Quality

Figure 7.1: Trade-off between time, cost and quality

This simple model does not consider any external influences which could impose further constraints on the project.

154

7.3   Agribusiness Activity Planning and Scheduling

7.3.1 The planning and scheduling environment

A number of sections should be considered in the planning and scheduling to encompass components of Figure 7.1, which include the following:

External factors
These are events and conditions that lie outside the control of the project management organization. Some of these factors can affect or completely wreck attempts at project planning. The following paragraphs list a few examples of the many possibilities.

Acts of God
An act of God is a legal term for events outside of human control and are associated with natural forces. Examples of acts of God include droughts, floods, pest and diseases which comes unexpectedly. A tree could fall on buildings or equipment causing damage. Lightning could set fire to homes and buildings. In many cases, insurance covers expense related to acts of God.

Fiscal policy
Fiscal policy, which is the policy of a national government in respect of taxation and other financial measures, can have a profound effect on projects and their planning. One extreme manifestation of this is when a government-funded project is cancelled or abandoned through a political decision (Food security projects are a prime example). Less immediate, but of more general concern, are the wider and longer term economic consequences of government policy. These can lead to project downscaling, delays and cancellations in all sectors of the industry.

Corporate strategy
Strategic decisions made by managers outside and above the project organization can affect many aspects of planning. Here are a few examples:

- A decision is made at the top management level of a group of companies to conduct a project in a different company within the group from that originally intended.

- A decision is made to delay the start of an internal project owing to diversion of funds for other purposes.

- A strategic decision is made to halt all new staff recruitment, so reducing the resources previously expected to be available for projects.

Statutory regulations

Legislation by national and regional governments can impose extra burdens on project designers which have to be taken into account at the planning stage. This can be particularly important feature of projects carried out in foreign countries, where the project manager would need to research the local employment, welfare, technical and commercial regulations before committing resources to a plan.

Working factors

These are most likely to affect the project manager and the project plans on a routine, day-to-day basis. Although responsibility for these factors usually lies with managers close to the project organization, they might be outside the control of the project manager, who has to learn to accept and plan accordingly.

Effective planning and scheduling, provide a sound basis for the project management progress. It should promote efficient working. Project personnel who are not constantly trying to overcome crises caused by bad planning can devote more their time to achieving the quality standards expected. A well-planned project stands a better chance of being completed on time and this, in turn, should contribute greatly to cost effectiveness and higher profitability.

7.3.2 Distinction between planning and scheduling

In project management terminology, some professional planners recognize that the words 'plan' and 'schedule' can have different meanings. We have found it convenient to observe the following distinction.

156

A plan can be considered as the listing or visual display that results when all project activities have been subjected to estimating, logical sequencing, target timing and the determination of priorities. For projects of any significant size, some form of network analysis is usually the preferred method for preparing a plan. However, some of the charting methods provide better visual aids and can be more effective for communicating plans to project personnel and are often quite adequate for small projects.

A schedule is obtained by doing additional work on the initial plan, so that resources needed to carry out all the project activities are taken into account. In other words, a schedule is the working document that results from matching the organization's available resources to the initial plan.

External factors

Acts of God

Fiscal policy

Corporate strategy

Market conditions

Statutory regulations

Working factors

Supporting services

Technical capability

Communications

Planning and scheduling

Attitudes and culture

Procedures and systems

Resources and capacity

Management skills

Organizational structure

Contributions to results

Quality

Safety
Reliability
Performance
Reputation

Time

Projects completed on time

Profitability

Costs held within budgets

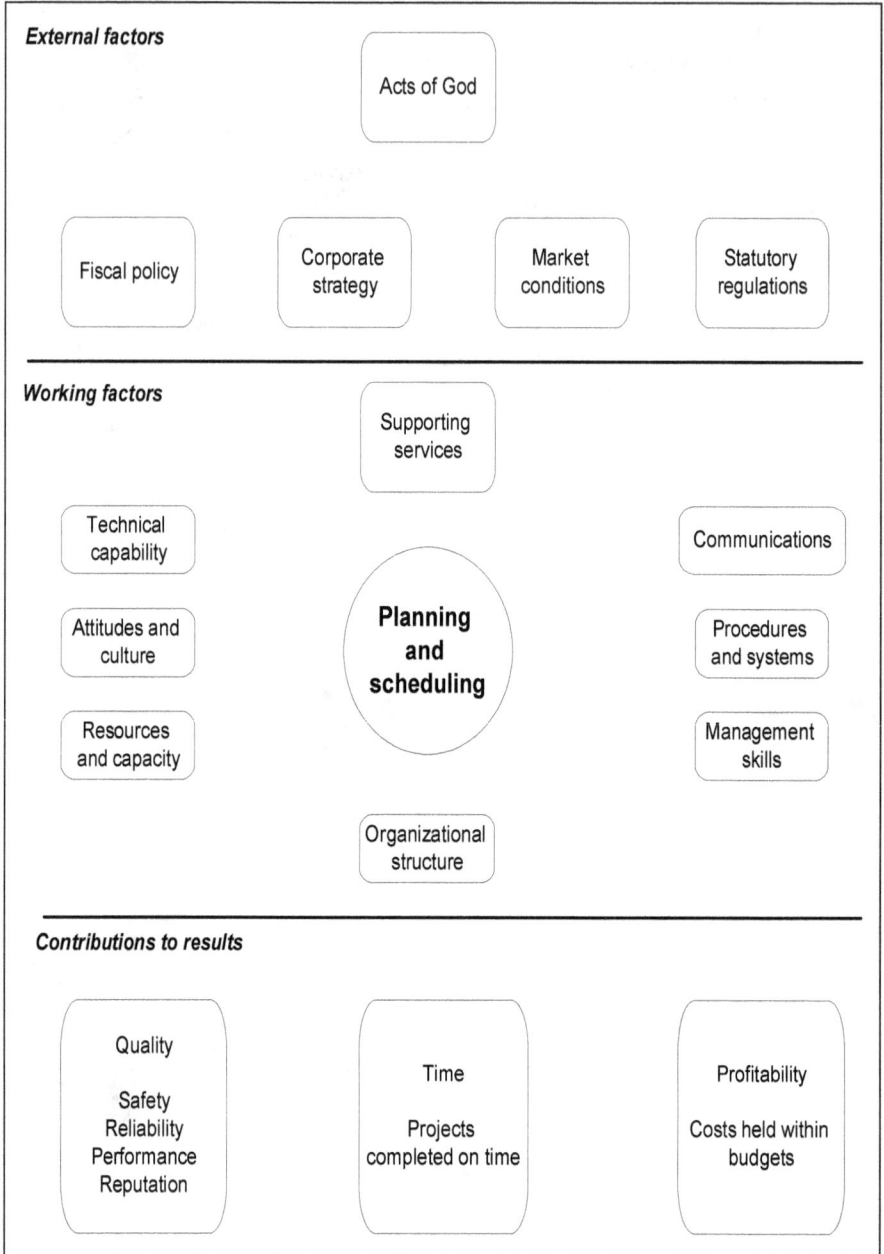

Figure 7.2: **Planning & Scheduling process**

7.3.3 The planning time frame

Planning (and scheduling) can be considered from two opposite viewpoints:

- A set of estimates of project activities is obtained and used to produce a plan that predicts a project completion date that is then accepted by everyone as the goal. Until this step in finished, the completion date is unknown. This is referred as the free planning approach.
- The end-date requirement is predetermined, governed by factors outside the planner's control. A delivery promise might already have been given to a customer in a sales proposal, or the project might have to be finished in time for a forthcoming exhibition or public event. This can be called the target – led planning approach.

The free planning approach

Schedules produced entirely from estimates, with no external pressure to compress the timescale, should allow the planner to develop a working schedule that is capable of being achieved with certainty. There is no need to overstretch any persons or resource in the project organization. This might be regarded by some as an ideal state of affairs. However, a new project plan made with no external pressure whatsoever will probably predict an end date that is ludicrous from the customer's point of view, destroying any possibility of gaining a valuable order.

Completely free planning, therefore, has its dangers. Pressure to find ways to expedite a project completion has potential pitfalls, because delays and stalling attract higher costs from fixed overheads and other causes. Giving planners complete freedom to dictate the project timescale might, therefore, not be quite so advisable.

Target-led planning

If a plan has to be suited to a predetermined target delivery requirement, all the estimates must be fitted into the available time frame as best they can. One temptation that must be resisted is for estimates to be shortened for no better reason than, that the time available is too short.

159

Another danger is removing all possible reserves (e.g. by planning to work overtime or seven days weekly) so that the plan is too tight and leaves no room for errors. Of course, it is sometimes possible to reduce time by allocating more resources, but the project manager should not be persuaded or coerced into trying to expedite a plan simply by marking down estimates without any justification. Any person will admit that projects planned on this basis are unlikely to be finished on time. Such optimistic plans can gain a temporary advantage by serving to pacify higher management or by deceiving a trusting customer into placing an order. Unfortunately the truth is bound to emerge sooner or later, bringing discredit to the project contractor.

Most planning is, however, time constrained. If the time available is restricted, particular ways have to be found for compressing the project timescale. One way is to examine the sequence of jobs and rearranged or overlap them to shorten the total time. A technique called fast tracking uses this approach but without creating unacceptable risks. Another approach is cost-time optimization. For maximum effect, fast tracking and cost-time optimization can be combined.

What happens if the targeted completion time for a new project is set later than necessary, so that the project plan is relaxed and stripped of all urgency? This would be rather unusual, but not impossible. Such extended schedules are an ideal breeding ground for budgetary excesses. According to Professor Parkinson's best-known law of pursuit of progress, work expands so as to fill the time available for its completion' (citation)

Resource limitations can complicate target-led planning. Problems occur because the initial plan is made without reference to available resources. Then, much later, work schedules are produced that are impossible to achieve, because the resources needed are either absent or are being used on other projects in the organization.

The ideal approach

In the best plans, the constituent elements are reliably estimated and arranged in their most logical sequence. Careful cooperation between the key participants in the proposed work is required, all striving to meet the needs of the customer and balancing these with the capabilities and resources of the project organization.

7.3.4 Benefits of project planning and control system

One of the main responsibilities of the project manager is to plan, track and control the project to meet pre-set objectives. To do this effectively, the project manger requires accurate and timely information. This information should be supplied by the project's planning and control system, which outlines the scope of work and measures performance against the original plan.

Agribusiness companies sometimes resist using project planning and control techniques because of the additional management costs. However, it should be appreciated that lack of information could be even more expensive if it leads to poor management decisions. Listed below are some of the main advantages associated with a fully integrated project planning and control system:

Estimating: The performance of the current project will form the estimating database for future projects. If this data is not collected by the planning and control system it may be lost forever.

Critical Path Method (CPM): CPM forces the managers to think about planning in a structured manner, whereby the critical activities serve as a guide to the degree of detail. The CPM presentation offers a tool for discussion with the other managers. Too much data but insufficient information may be generated on a regular basis if the reports are not structured and summarized properly. CPM can be used to provide focused information.

Project system integration: The planning and control system can provide the link between the project and corporate reporting systems. Without this link double processing may be necessary to satisfy the information needs of both systems.

Response time: Timely response on project performance is essential for effective project control. The planning and control system can adjust the feedback to address the needs of the project. However, with corporate systems that haves accounts departments set up in monthly reporting cycles where feedback on invoices, for example, may be 4 to 6 weeks behind the current time, various project components would have to be synchronized.

Reporting interfaces: The planning and control system's data base can be structured around the Work Breakdown Structure (WBS) for project reporting and around the Organization Breakdown Structure (OBS) for corporate reporting. Without this integrated system, the two reporting requirements would have to be processed separately.

Trends: Projects are best controlled by monitoring the progress trends of time, cost and performance. This information may not be available to the project manager if the trend parameters are derived from a number of functional sources.

Data Capture: If the project progress reporting is based on information supplied by the functional departments, the project manager cannot control the accuracy of this information. The problem here is that it may only become obvious that the reporting is inaccurate towards the end of the project, when it could be too late to bring the project back on course to meet its objectives.

Responsibility: If the project manager is to be held as the single point of responsibility, his authority should be commensurate with this position. Therefore, when the project manager accepts this responsibility, he needs authority over the supply of project information.

Cost of mistakes: To implement a fully integrated project management system will certainly increase the project office budget. However, without an effective planning and control system the cost of mistakes due to lack of adequate control may be even higher.

Procedures: The planning and control system enables the project manager to develop procedures and work instructions tailored to the specific needs of the project.

Client: The project manager is the project's single point of responsibility and the company's representative to the client. When holding meetings with a client, the planning and control system will provide information about every aspect of the project.

The above points outline the benefits of an independent project management planning and control system to give the project manager the best opportunity to effectively plan, monitor and control the project.

Unfortunately, it is not always possible to substantiate these benefits financially as many of them like good customer service are intangible.

7.4 Bar Charts and Gantt Charts

Bar charts derived from Gantt charts, named after their originator, the American industrial engineer Henry Gantt (1861-1919)have long been in widespread use and continue to be very valuable planning aids. Bar charts are not only easy to draw or construct and interpret but are readily adaptable to a great variety of planning requirements.

With the advent of more sophisticated planning methods, notably critical path network analysis, bar charts fell into undeserved disrepute. Although more modern techniques must be preferred in many cases, the older charting methods still have their valuable uses. Planning by bar charts is infinitely better than no planning at all.

The visual impact of a well-displayed schedule can be a powerful aid to controlling a simple project. Bar charts are still preferred to other methods in many agribusiness project sites. All levels of supervision and management find them convenient as day-to-day control tools. Even when projects have been planned with advanced computer techniques, the same computer systems are often used to plot the schedule data as bar charts for day-to-day use.

Figure 7. indicates the format of a Gantt bar chart, where the top and base are calendar time-scale in days (1) and the activities (2) are listed on the left. The scheduling of each activity is represented by a horizontal line (3), from the activity's start to finish date. The length of the activity line is proportional to its estimated duration.

Once the project has started, the Gantt chart can further be used as a tool for project control. This is achieved by drawing a second line under the planned schedule to indicate activity progress (4). The relative position of the progress line to the planned line indicates percentage complete and remaining duration, while the relative position between the progress line and time now (5) indicates actual progress against planned progress. The benefits of the Gantt chart can be clearly seen. Not only are the calculations simple but it combines all the above information on one page.

7.5 Network Diagrams

For a project plan to be effective it must equally address the parameters of activity time and network logic. As project became larger and more complex, the Gantt chart was found to be lacking as a planning and control tool because it could not indicate the logical relationships between activities. This logical relationship is required to model the effect schedule variance will have down-stream in the project.

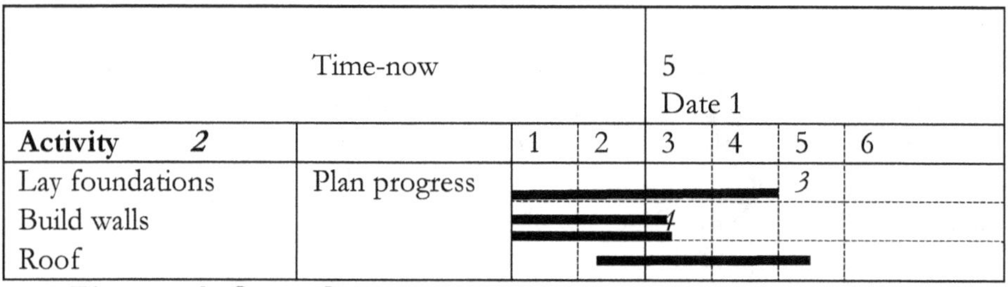

Time-now							5 Date 1	
Activity *2*		1	2	3	4	5	6
Lay foundations	Plan progress					*3*	
Build walls				*1*			
Roof							

Figure 7.3: Gantt Chart

In the 1950's, feedback from industry and commerce indicated that project cost and time overruns were all too common. It was suggested at the time that the project estimates were on the optimistic side in order to gain work. However, a more important reason emerged which indicated that the planning and control techniques, available to manage large complex projects were inadequate.

With these short comings in mind, network planning techniques were developed by Charles Flagle, the US Navy and using one of the first commercial computers, the Remington Rand Univac. Flagle wrote a paper in 1956 on 'Probability based tolerances in forecasting and planning'. Although it was not published in the Journal of Industrial Engineers until April 1961, it was in a sense the forerunner of the US Navy's Program Evaluation and Review Technique (PERT). Both PERT and Remington Rand Univac's Critical Path Method (CPM) used a similar network format, where the activities are presented in boxes and the sequence of the activities from left to right show the logic of the project.

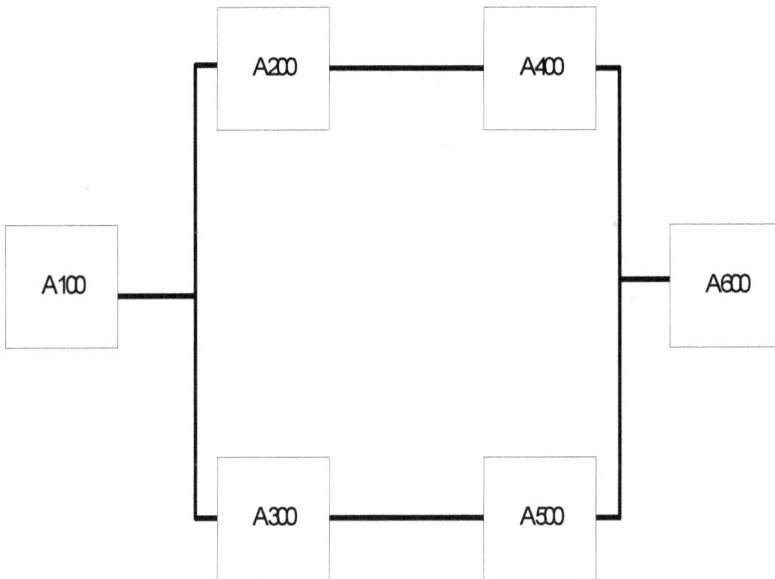

Figure 7.4 Network Diagram

7.5.1 *Activity duration*

The main difference between PERT and CPM was how they addressed activity time durations. The accuracy of an activity's time estimate usually depends on the information available from previous projects. If an activity has been performed before, its duration should be accurately predicted. However, activities with a new scope of work, which are difficult to measure or are dependent on other uncertain variables, may have a range of possible time durations.

CPM uses a deterministic approach, which suits a project whose time durations can be accurately predicted e.g. a construction project. PERT, on the other hand, uses a probabilistic approach, which suits a project whose time durations may vary over a range of possibilities, e.g. a research project.

7.5.2 PERT

The PERT technique was developed to apply a statistical treatment to the possible range of activity time durations. A three time probabilistic model was developed, using pessimistic, optimistic and most likely time durations. The three time scenarios were imposed on a normal distribution to calculate the activity's expected time.

For PERT, three time estimates are required for every activity:

t_o = the most optimistic duration that could be foreseen

t_m = the most likely duration

t_p = the most pessimistic duration

From these quantities a probable duration is calculated for each activity, on a statistical basis, assuming that the errors will fall within a normal distribution curve when all the project activities are taken as the sample.

The expected time is:

$$t_e = \frac{t_o + 4t_m + t_p}{6}$$

This calculation is repeated on all activities in the network and used to predict the probability of completing the project within the scheduled time. When more than about a hundred separate activities are included in the network, a computer becomes necessary to remove the drudgery from the calculations and enable the results to be made available in time for appropriate action to be taken.

Some authorities do not accept that the normal distribution curve is suitable for predicting the spread of estimating errors. It is well known that estimates are frequently too optimistic rather than too pessimistic. Whichever statistical basis is chosen, PERT will produce a critical path in the same way as any other network analysis method.

The success of the Polaris Submarine project helped the establishment of PERT in the 1960s as a planning tool within many large corporations. There were, however, a number of basic problems, which reduced PERT's effectiveness and eventually led to its fall from popularity. These included:

Statistical analysis was not generally understood by project managers. Computer technology limitations; batch card input, and systems were not interactive and had a slow response.

PERT is currently enjoying a renaissance as a tool to address risk management.

7.5.3 Critical Path Method

The Critical Path Method (CPM) was developed in 1957 and used on a Remington Rand Univac as a management tool to improve the planning and control of a construction project to build a processing plant for the Du Pont Corporation. CPM was initially set-up to address the time cost trade-off dilemma often presented to project managers, where there is a complex relationship between the project time to complete and cost to complete. CPM enables the planner to model the effect various project time cycles have on direct and indirect costs. Shortening the project duration will reduce indirect costs, but may increase the direct cost. This technique is often called project crashing or acceleration.

The initial growth of CPM in the industrial market was slow, due to the lack of project management education and CPM training offered at the time by the universities and colleges. The early differences between CPM and PERT have largely disappeared, and it is now common to use the two terms interchangeable as a generic name to include the whole planning and control process.

7.5.4 ADM and PDM

There are two basic networking techniques:

- Arrow Diagram Method (ADM) also called Network-On-Arrow, and
- Precedence Diagram Method (PDM)

167

The basic difference between the two network diagrams is that with ADM the activity information is written on the arrow or rational link, while in PDM the activity information is positioned in the node or box. After carrying out the activity calculations, both methods will produce exactly the same result.

There are many practitioners who swear by their preference whether it is ADM or PDM. To be fair, both techniques have their benefits. Noting market trends, PDM has now established itself as the most popular planning technique, especially since recently introduced project management software have adopted PDM as their standard.

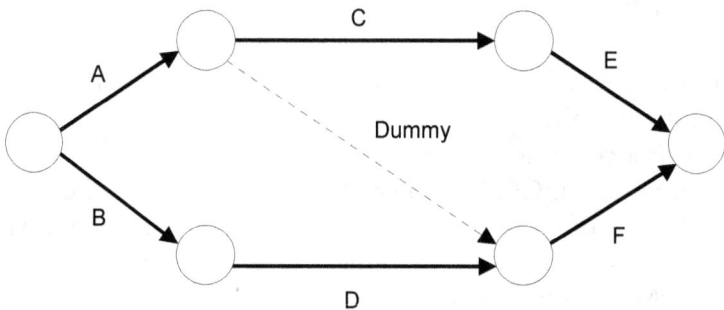

Arrow Diagram method

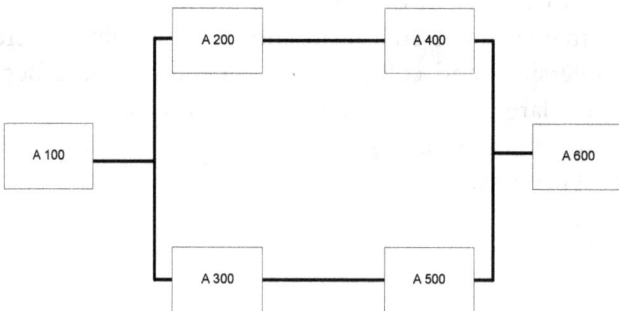

Precedence Diagram method

Figure 7.5: Two Basic Networking Techniques

7.5.5 Critical Path Analysis Using Arrow Diagrams

The heart of any activity-on-arrow system is the arrow diagram, logic diagram or 'network' itself. This differs from the more familiar bar chart in several important respects. Arrow diagrams, in common with all other network methods are not drawn to scale. Every network is, however, constructed with careful thought to show as accurately as possible the logical relationships and interdependence of each activity or task with all the other activities in the project. Indeed, it is for this reason that networks are sometimes called logic diagrams.

Jargon

The strange terms have their origins in the mathematical theory of networks. In this alternative language, the circles are termed as nodes and the arrows become arcs. The first event circle of an activity (the preceding event) is called the node for that activity, and the end event circle (the succeeding event) is called its J node. Arrow networks are occasionally referred to, therefore, as IJ networks. This jargon is by no means essential to the understanding and application of project network analysis, but the terms crop up occasionally in the literature.

Activities and events in arrow diagram

Figure 7.6 shows a very simple arrow diagram. Each circle represents a project event. An event might be the start of a project, the start of an activity (or task), the completion of a task or the end of a project. The arrow joining any two events represents the activity or task that must take place before the second event can be declared as achieved. Events are usually shared between tasks, so that a single event might signal the completion of several tasks and the start of one or several more tasks. In the figure it is obvious, therefore, that seven activities link eight events.

Each circle represents a project event, such as the start or finish of a project activity. The arrow joining any two events denotes the activity or time needed for the project to progress from one event to the next. The numbers inside the circles are put there to identify the events. Activities are identified by their preceding and succeeding event numbers, so that the central activity in this example would be called activity 4 to 5. No activity can start until all activities leading into its start event have been completed. In this example activity 4 to 5 cannot be started until event 4 has been achieved or, in other words, until activities 1 to 4, 2 to 4 and 3 to 4 have all been completed. Similarly no activity following event 5 can start until activity 4 to 5 is finished. Networks do not need to be drawn to any timescale and the length of an arrow has no significance.

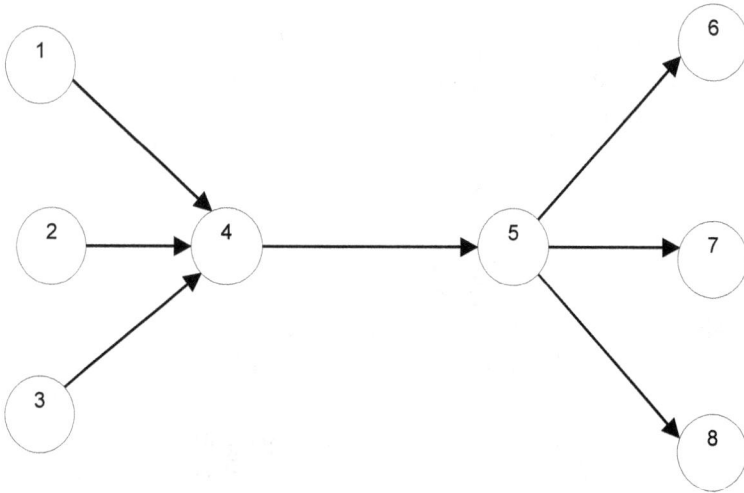

Figure 7.6: The Main Elements of Arrow Network Logic

Direction

By convention, activity arrows are drawn from left to right. This means that the arrowheads are not strictly necessary and could be omitted. Occasionally, perhaps when a network is altered or through lack of space on a page, it might be impossible to avoid drawing an arrow going vertically or even from right to left. In those exceptional cases the arrowheads must be shown so that there can be no ambiguity about the direction of any arrow.

Scale

Unlike bar charts, network diagrams are not drawn to any scale. The length of the arrows and size of the event circles have no significance whatsoever.

Identification number in arrow diagrams

The numbers in the event circles are there simply to label the events: they allow the events and their associated activities to be referred to without ambiguity. In Figure 7.6, the arrow from event 1 to event 4, for example, can be described as activity 1 to 4.

Logical dependencies and constraints in arrow diagrams

In any arrow diagram, no event can be considered complete until all activities leading into it have been finished. Likewise, no activity can start until its preceding event has been achieved. This point can be demonstrated by reference to Figure 7.6. Event 4 cannot be considered as being reached or achieved until all three activities leading into it from the left have been achieved. When event 4 has been achieved, but not before, activity 4 to 5 can start. Activities 5 to 6, 5 to 7 and 5 to 8 must all wait until activity 4 to 5 has been finished before they can start.

Now applying the arrow diagram method to an everyday 'agribusiness project', suppose it is planned to plant a mango tree in the mango orchard. If an arrow diagram were to be drawn, the result would look something like the sequence shown in the figure below. The interdependence of activities is clear in this case, and only one sequence of events is possible. The tree cannot be placed in the hole before the hole has been dug, and there would be little point in filling in the hole before putting in the tree.

Activity duration estimates and descriptions

Estimates for the duration of each activity have been made for the simple tree project, as follows:

Activity	Description	Estimated duration
1 to 2	Dig the hole	20 minutes
2 to 3	Position the tree	1 minute
3 to 4	Fill in the hole	5 minutes

No one needs network analysis to realize that this project is going to take a minimum of 26 minutes to complete. Notice, however, that the estimated duration is written above each activity arrow, with a concise activity description written below. Space on networks is usually limited so experienced planners become adept at describing tasks in the least possible number of words.

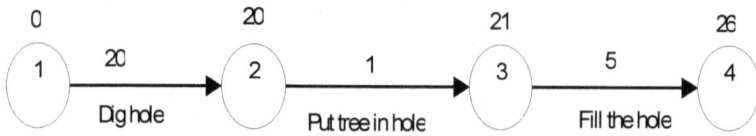

Figure 7.7: Tree Project Network Using Arrow Notation

The numbers written above the activity arrows in this simple example show the estimated duration of each project task. Minutes have been used in this case but any time units can be used provided that the same units are used throughout the network. Days or weeks would be more usual units for an industrial or commercial agribusiness project. The numbers written above the events circles are calculated by adding the estimated activity durations from left to right. They show the earliest possible time by which each event could be achieved.

Example 1: Consider the following table, which gives a list of activities involved in an agro-based factory expansion scheme.

Activity	Preceding activity
A: Plan new site	–
B: Move to temporary premises	A
C: Build new plant	A
D: Train staff	B
E: Install machinery	C
F: Move production to new site	D, E

This table describes the precedence for each activity. For instance, activity A (plan new site) is preceded by nothing. Activity C is preceded by A. This tells us that the new plant cannot be built (activity C) before the new site has been planned (activity A). Activity F is preceded by both D and E. This implies that the production will be moved to the new site (activity F) only after staff have been trained (D) and machinery installed (E). Following the description of lists activities above, draw the natural diagram.

Dummy activities

The network in Figure 7.8 below represents a slightly more complex project. Now the configuration is actually seen to be a network of activities, and not just a simple straight-line sequence. In this example, as in all real project networks, there is more than one path through the arrows to project completion. In fact, there are three possible routes here to the final event 6, one of which flows through the dotted arrow linking event 4 to event 3.

Dummy activities do not represent actual work and practically always have zero duration. Rather, they denote a constraint or line of dependence between different activities. In the figure, therefore, the start of activity 3 to 6 is dependent not only upon completion of activity 2 to 3, but it must also await completion of activity 1 to 4. Alternatively expressed, activity 3 to 6 cannot start until events 3 to 4 have both been achieved.

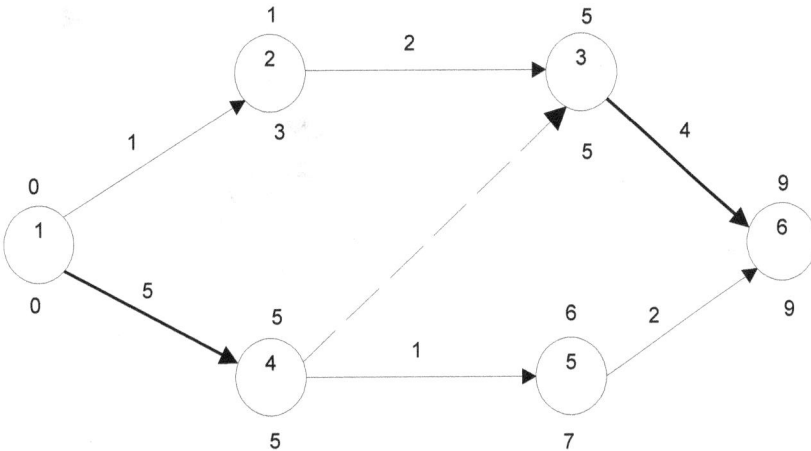

Figure 7.8: Arrow Network Time Analysis

Example 1:   Consider the following list of activities:

Activity	Preceding activity
A	-
B	-
C	B
D	A
E	A,C

One attempt at drawing a network of these activities, albeit as a Gantt chart, could be that shown in Figure 7.9 below.

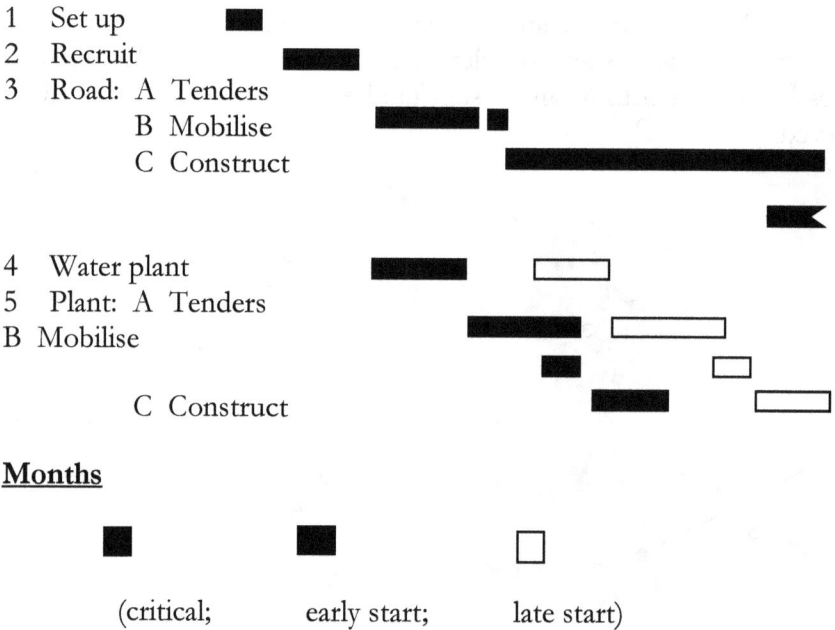

1   Set up
2   Recruit
3   Road: A Tenders
          B Mobilise
          C Construct

4   Water plant
5   Plant: A Tenders
B Mobilise

          C Construct

Months

(critical;   early start;   late start)

Figure 7.9: Bar Chart for Phased Expenditure

The dotted arrow in this network is a dummy activity. As already seen in the tree project, numbers written above event circles show the earliest possible time by which events can be achieved, calculated by adding all the activity durations from left to right. Where there is more than one possible path, the longest must determine the earliest possible event time. In this case, the earliest time for event 3 is dependent on the path through the dummy. The numbers below the event circles have been found by subtracting activity durations from right to left from the final event, again taking the longest path. These numbers are the latest permissible times by which each event must be achieved if the completion time for the whole project is not to be delayed.

Time units for activity duration

In the figure (as in the simple tree project), numbers have been written above the activity arrows to show their estimated durations. The units used are always chosen by the planner as being the most suitable for the project. In the tree project or network, minutes were the most appropriate unit of time, but days or weeks are the units most often used for project plans. The best modern computer programs will, however, accept any unit of time for seconds to years.

The forward pass

In the project network, the earliest possible time for each event, and finally, the earliest possible time for project completion at event 6 has been calculated by adding activity duration estimates along the arrows from left to right. This is always the first step in the full time analysis of any network and is known as the 'forward pass'.

The forward pass process is more complicated in this than it was in the simple tree project because there is more than one possible path through the network. The earliest time indicated for each event appears to depend on which path is followed, but only the longest preceding path will give the correct result. The earliest possible completion time for event 3, for instance, might seem to be $1 + 2 = 3$, if the path through events 1, 2 and 3 is taken. Event 3 cannot be achieved, however, until the end of week 5 because of the longer path through the dummy. This also means that the earliest possible start time for activity 3 to 6 is the end of week 5 (or, for more practical purposes, the beginning of week 6).

Thus the earliest possible time for any event is found by adding the estimated durations of all preceding activities along the path that produces the greatest time. By following this procedure through the network to the end of the project at event 6 it emerges that the earliest possible estimated project completion time is nine weeks.

The backward pass

Now consider event 5 in the figure. Its earliest possible achievement time is the end of week 6, three weeks before the earliest possible time for finishing the project at event 6. It is clear that activity 5 to 6, which is only expected to last for two weeks, could be delayed for up to one week without upsetting the overall timescale. In other words, although the earliest possible achievement time for event 5 is week 6, its latest permissible achievement time is the end of week 7. This result can be indicated on the arrow diagram by writing the latest permissible time underneath the event circle. The result is found this time, not by addition from left to right along the arrows, but in the opposite way by subtracting the estimated durations of activities from right to left ($9 - 2 = 7$ for event 5).

This subtraction exercise can be repeated throughout the network, writing the latest permissible times below all the event circles. Where more than one path exists, the longest must be chosen so that the result after subtraction gives the smallest remainder. This is illustrated at event 4 where the correct subtraction route lies through the dummy.

Although the earliest and latest times are written above and below the event circles, they can also be applied to the activities leading into and out of the events. Thus, for example, activity 5 to 6 has:

- Estimated duration: 2 weeks
- Earliest possible start: end of week 6 (beginning of week 7)
- Earliest possible finish (6+2): end of week 8
- Latest permissible finish: end of week 9
- Total float (9-8): 1 week

The term float indicates the amount of leeway available for starting and finishing an activity. The word slack is also used sometimes).

Critical path

When all the earliest possible and latest permissible times have been added to the diagram, there will be at least one chain of events from the start of the network to the end where the earliest and latest event times are the same, indicating zero float. These events are critical to the successful achievement of the whole project within its earliest possible time. The route joining these events is not surprisingly termed the critical path. Although all activities may be important, it is the critical activities that must claim priority for resources and for management attention.

Examples and Exercises

The Figure 7.10 shows a network with 12 activities (A, B, C,.M) and 7 events. The figures on the arrows are the duration of the activities labelled as arbitrary units. Activity E is a dummy. How many paths are there through the network and what are their duration? Find the minimum project time, the critical activities and the total float for each non-critical activity.

What are the critical activities and minimum project time if:

a) the dummy is removed
b) the duration of M is increased to 15 units.

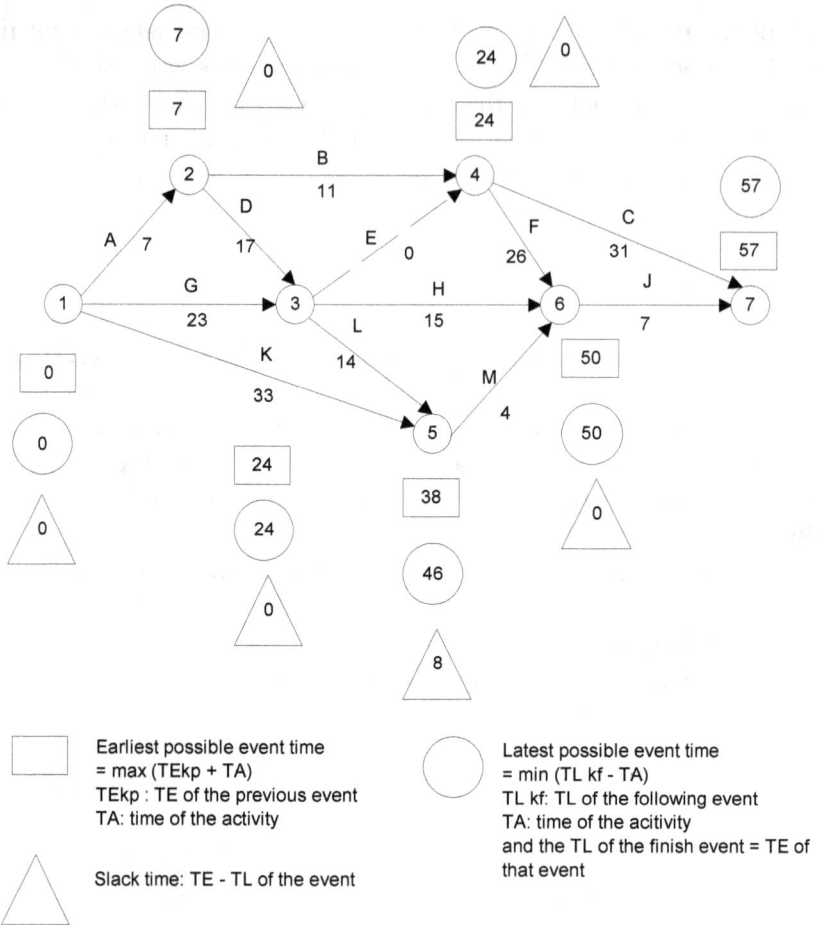

Earliest possible event time
= max (TEkp + TA)
TEkp : TE of the previous event
TA: time of the activity

Latest possible event time
= min (TL kf - TA)
TL kf: TL of the following event
TA: time of the acitivity
and the TL of the finish event = TE of that event

Slack time: TE - TL of the event

The critical path is given by the activities relying the events for which TE = TL or whereby the slack equals zero.

Example
TE of event 2 is 0+ 2= 2
TE of event 3 is 0 + 23=23
TE of event 5 is Max (0+ 33 and 24 + 14) = 38

TL of event 7 is TE of event 7 is 57
TL of event 6 is 57 - 7 = 50
TL of event 4 is Min (57 - 31 and 50 - 26) = 24

Minimum project time: 57 days
Critical path: A - D - E - F - J

Figure 7.10: The Determination of Critical Path

Other exercises:

1. Assume that you are letting a contract for widening a farm access road. Draw a PERT diagram for the activities from the start of preparation of specifications until the contractor go-ahead. Determine the critical path and the shortest time to complete the set of tasks.

   Prepare a table showing the earliest start time, earliest finish time, latest start time, latest finish time, and slack time for each activity.

Table 7.1: Example of PERT Drawing Process

Task	Description	Expected time (working days)	Immediate predecessors
A	Prepare specifications for job	5	None
B	Notify property owners	2	None
C	Select prospective bidders	4	None
D	Contact prospective bidders	4	C
E	Send out requests for bid	3	A, D
F	Hold a bid conference	2	E
G	Secure property owners approval	14	B
H	Wait for bidders to prepare bids	10	F
I	Receive bids	2	H
J	Evaluate bids	5	I
K	Prepare final job schedule	2	G, J
L	Arrange details with water company	4	G, J
M	Notify selected bidders	1	K
N	Negotiate and sign contract	2	L, M
	Go-ahead for contractor	0	N

Construct a PERT diagram for the following information, anddetermine the critical path.

Activity	To	Tm	Tp	Immediate predecessors
A	1	2	4	None
B	2	4	6	A
C	2	6	10	A
D	6	8	10	B
E	4	6	8	C
F	6	10	14	C
G	8	10	12	D, E
H	12	14	16	F
I	4	8	12	G, H
J	10	12	16	G, H
K	2	4	6	I
L	6	10	14	J

Assuming that the schedule allows 40 days to complete the whole project, calculate the probability of completion by the scheduled date.

The contractor wants to quote a scheduled completion date that would give him a 90 percent chance of attainment. How many days should he allow in his schedule?

7.6 Managing Money

Money – or the lack of it – is one of the most frequently cited limitations in development, as a reason for delays, poor performance, and lack of maintenance. Even the other great bugbear – lack of skills – can ultimately be traced back to lack of funds for training and the appointment of top quality personnel, and, further back still, to a lack of funds for the education that underpins all training. The content of this chapter partly concerns the problems of managing money from the point of view of the manager of a typical development project operated by government staff or parastatal agencies and of NGO's (although NGOs typically are not trading or banking organizations); such organizations normally provide funds to cover expenditure, and require revenues to be returned to the central administration, so that the commercial problem of financing expenditure from cash flow plus borrowings does not arise.

Money management has two key aspects – setting targets and interpreting feedback; the following sections explore these in more detail.

7.6.1 Phasing expenditure budgets

One of the most difficult set of circumstances in which to plan expenditure is undoubtedly that of the development project. The more complex the project, and the more agencies are involved, the more potential for delays and unforeseen obstacles . However, the same fundamental principles apply for all such projects: expenditure is the result of physical activity, not its cause. That is, you have to plan physical activity and deduce financial activity from it; however, having done this, you may well find that overall progress is restricted by the 'money' resource. Hence, the implementation scheduling sequence unfolds like this:

- Compile an activity network to get a complete list of activities in a proper sequence.
- Draft a preliminary implementation plan.
- Carry out any resource level-line necessary to ease peak demands for physical resources and personnel.
- Carry out any necessary 'crashing' to shorten the programme.
- Work out the rates of expenditure that result.
- If the rate of expenditure exceeds the available budget, revise the physical programme (i.e. the second step above) and repeat, bearing in mind the need to give priority to funds for critical activities.

Money is a slightly peculiar resource in three ways. Firstly, virtually all activities compete for it. Secondly, many activities generate a stream of costs that run on after the activity itself ceases. For example, hiring staff generates a near-unstoppable stream of salary and welfare costs; renting premises similarly generates a stream of bills for rent (and usually for utilities); installing plant generates a stream of maintenance costs, which, however, are often ignored in contravention. Thirdly, the pattern of money requirement is often much less even than the pattern of say, labour requirement. For example, payments for a piece of imported plant might be 15% on signature of contract, 15% on port clearance, two phased payments of 20% during installation, and the remainder divided between a payment on completion and a retention to cover defects appearing during the first season. Similarly, civil engineering and building works will generate a flow of staged payments (and occasionally, loans for the purchase of a specialist plant), usually with a distinct peak in the middle of the contract when the project is busiest. These make it difficult to level money requirements in the same way as can be done for labour. The trial-and-error approach is often used; and some of the more sophisticated computer programmes offer facilities for treating finance as a resource.

The principles of the central step of this process – creating a phased expenditure forecast – are demonstrated using a simple example. It might not be a bad idea to repeat the working of this yourself.

The project centres on the upgrading of an existing abattoir, necessitating the construction of a plant to take in live cattle, sheep and goats; produce clean carcasses and offals; and convert most offal, blood, and other waste into feed-quality blood and bone meals. The plant is integral with its prefabricated shell, but a new water supply is required and is to be installed to supply water during construction. A programme of road improvement was included in the scheme, mainly to handle an anticipated increase of output of meat in refrigerated transport (the increase being largely attributable to a separate and now successful initiative to encourage stall-feeding); however, the existing road is not adequate for access for construction.

7.6.2   Interpreting expenditure data

In general, projects will have three expenditure lines: the early start expenditure line, the late start expenditure line, and the planned expenditure line. Expenditure control and monitoring is   crucially important: it is necessary to ensure that money is spent in accordance with the parameters of the authorizations given. Unexpected large deviations from the plan may suggest the need to consult funding agencies (donor, treasury, the NGO's sponsors) about either anticipated over-expenditure or anticipated delay of expenditure resulting from changes in the pattern of physical activity.

Expenditure data is not a good management tool in itself. Even if the obvious pitfalls are avoided (e.g. comparing actual expenditure on bills paid basis with a plan made on sums committed basis), there is a fundamental flaw in the idea of expenditure rate as a primary monitoring tool. This arises from the distinction between expenditure on critical items and expenditure on non-critical items. It is tempting to assume that if the cumulative expenditure graph is used as a control chart, and actual expenditure plotted on it, when the 'actual' line stays between the early start and late start cost lines, then all is well; and that when it returns into the zone between those two lines after having fallen below it, then successful remedial action has been taken. Neither assumption is reliable – in fact, the latter is almost totally fallacious.

Consider the case of a project to build a facility for producing fingerlings. The critical path ran through the construction of ponds, and the production of the great grandparent and parent generations of fish – but the Fisheries Department's construction team concentrated on building the headquarters' offices and library. As these were costly structures, the disbursement rates looked fine – but in terms of advancing the project towards production, virtually zero progress was being made. And, of course, the same applies with even more force to the situation where a low rate of expenditure is being pushed up over a relatively short period. The easiest way to do this is to bring forward non-critical expenditure.

These considerations make no sense with regard to the practice in many government departments of using disbursement rates (i.e. expenditure actually made, as a percentage of planned expenditure) as an early warning device. On operational items i.e. regular expenditure on fuel, foodstuffs, and so on, for an established enterprise, the relative rate of expenditure is a useful control tool.

A slightly better approach is to use expenditure rate on critical activities only – but to do this properly means knowing the current structure of the project, in terms of where the critical and non-critical paths actually lie. Given this knowledge, the sensible thing to do is to monitor physical activity, and report its impact on financial matters rather than to use expenditure as a poor proxy measure of progress.

7.6.3   Financial records

The financial records required for controlling 'official' expenditure are relatively simple, although there may be a large volume of them on a big project. For each expenditure heading, a record of the form shown in Fig 7.10 is needed:

183

Project.............		Expenditure heading................................			
Date	Item	Amount Committed	Balance	Amount Paid	Remarks

Figure 7.11: Expenditure Record

The record is identified with the project name, the heading (e.g. Miombo Fisheries Project, Building Programme 2012/13), and the sum allocated is written on the top line of the 'balance' column. As expenditure is committed, it is entered – and, periodically, the balance remaining available for expenditure is reduced by the running total of the amounts committed. It is, of course, committed expenditure that you have to watch. Amounts paid are also entered when the transaction is complete, and a remark column allows the rewarding of voucher numbers and comments on any unusual factors of the transaction.

7.6.4 Budgetary methods

So far, we have focused on expenditure budgets for individual projects, how physical activity can be tailored to fit within budgetary limits, the ways in which financial data can be collected, and its limitations as a control tool. However, there is another side of the budgetary story: how allocations get made in the first place. This affects managers, and they, in turn, affect the process.

Looking at the national level first, budgeting is a heavily constrained process: there is always a very sizeable burden of costs resulting from earlier decisions that cannot readily be disposed of. Existing contracts, essential imports, and the salaries of government employees can mop up a very large slice of national income, leaving only a small percentage available for discretionary spending, particularly on new developments. As a result, much budgetary decision-making is essentially incremental, that is, marginal modifications and additions to an existing base. Attempts have been made to introduce zero-base budgeting (ZBB) in large governmental organizations (e.g. Ministry of Agriculture and Food Security); under this system, in theory, there is no unchallengeable base of expenditure whose necessity is taken for granted, and every significant expenditure has to be justified. It is very difficult to establish a rational basis for the relative proportions of money to be spent on vocational education, soil conservation policy, enforcing plant quarantine regulations, and extension – and impossible to repeat the exercise within the confines of each year's budgetary timetable.

As a result, successful introduction of zero-based budgets could open up a whole series of internal conflicts about the relative size of allocations, which usually result from combinations of historical accident and political pressure. ZBB has other costs too – notably the deterioration in morale caused by the way it appears to threaten jobs and pet projects. This is not to say that periodic review of the usefulness of major sectors of official expenditure should not be made; however, this is a process that should be separate from the annual budgetary exercise.

This exercise is far from being a straightforward technical one. Normally starting from the very top, a formal request for preparation of the annual budget will be made; this will usually indicate the acceptable change on the previous year, often (for reasons similar to those that limit the scope of ZBB) on the across board basis. For example, the amounts budgeted for salaries may not exceed 103% of the previous year's amounts, or that capital expenditure must not exceed 95% of previous year's amount. One item that will be tabulated separately is the annual development budget (ADB), under which much of the discretionary margin between national income expenditure (adjusted by any planned deficit) is spent.

The consequences of loss of credibility of managers' budgets in the eyes of financial administrators are both specific and general. Specific in the sense that, if you want to succeed with a plea for additional funds to cope with unforeseen problems, people have to believe that your request is realistic. General in the sense that poor project management makes, in aggregate, a significant contribution to the uncertainty of the budgetary process. An interesting study of this topic suggested that the two parameters that determine the pattern of budgetary behaviour are wealth and variability in the level of income and outgoings. The following classification is based on this idea:

(i)   Rich, but uncertain (the oil states at the height of the boom) work by grant budgeting – there is so much money available that any reasonable (and some unreasonable) proposals will be approved; this process occasionally "breaks the bank" and various crisis management measures are then adopted.

(ii)   Rich, but certain (developed countries except in times of recession) work by incremental budgeting – the revenue is known, and a relatively tidy version of the budgetary process outlined above is operated with relatively generous and predictable development funding which is not usually subject to revision during the financial year; choice of developments is usually made on an incremental basis.

(iii) Poor but certain (many local government authorities in all parts of the world) work by revenue budgeting, with most of the emphasis placed on making sure that commitments stay within the bounds of anticipated income.

(iv)   Poor and uncertain (most developing countries) work by iterative budgeting. Both income and expenditure are highly unstable. In the case of income, this results from economic weakness and reliance on climate-dependent primary products. In the case of expenditure, it results from the relative importance of inherently uncertain development work, aggravated by poor physical and financial management skills. As a consequence, attempts to operate a tidy budgeting scheme fail. Drastic revisions – usually cut-backs – have to be made during the financial year, regardless of their impact on part-completed work. In extreme situations, government delays payment on its purchases, with the results that prices get pushed up and suppliers become unhelpful. In some circumstances, government payment orders are sold at a discount to traders and financiers by suppliers anxious to realize some proceeds to stay in business.

It can be established that the contorted, multi-layered controls on expenditure often found in developing countries are there for reasons other than incompetence and 'cultural' love of red tape – and that development and its management themselves make a contribution to the problem.

7.7 Problem Areas in Project Implementation

All projects have problems, which may be large or relatively minor. The ways by which problems occur vary from project to project, but principally they fall into certain well-defined areas. These are briefly summarized as follow:

Institutional problems. These arise when authority, responsibilities, or working relationships are not fully clarified, with formal and properly applied lines of communication and decision-making among the project teams and the organizational units are out of sync. For example, in a large regional development project, difficulties in obtaining land and water for production ponds for every interested farmer may be the result of dealing with the wrong government organization, poor project management and staffing, equipment procurement difficulties, and poor monitoring and evaluation.

Conceptual problems. These arise from inadequacies in project formulation, resulting from insufficient background studies, errors in analysis or inadequacies in the planning work to be performed. For example, in a project to introduce improved agricultural practices to subsistence farmers in a developing country, the concepts may be too flexible, the objectives wrong or non-sustainable, project components may be too numerous or too large, or the schedule may be unrealistic.

Technical problems; Such problems usually arise from unexpected factors discovered during project implementation or errors in project implementation work. For example, in a project to convert traditional fish production ponds into shrimp ponds, there might be a consistent shortfall in production of shrimp due to seasonal water quality changes and a low-quality feed not foreseen in project formulation. Or the standard of engineering design and/or construction to deepen the ponds and exchange more water may be poor.

Financial problems: These arise when procedures and schedules for funds, manpower, supplies, and equipment, etc. necessary to carry out project activities have not been adequately organized.

Alternatively, delays in implementation result in additional costs, or project costs have been-under estimated. For example, in a large project to clear mangrove for shrimp production ponds, there may be recurrent budget shortages due to poor scheduling of heavy earth-moving equipment for digging new canals or dredging, or as a result, under-estimated investment or operational costs. Financial problems may also occur because of sudden changes in the price of feed or the market value of the products, all as a result of competition or other market factors. Drawing from previous chapters, mangrove clearing for shrimp farming, while common, also has high environmental costs.

Social problems: Such problems often result from inadequacies in the analysis of social aspects of the project in formulation work, or from changes in social balances or social organization during project implementation. For example, in a project to introduce aquaculture to traditional coastal fishermen, problems may be manifested by slow adoption of farming techniques by the fishermen who may find aquaculture less attractive and more difficult than fishing. Alternatively, there may be an inequitable distribution of benefits as some sites (farms) are naturally more productive than others.

Political problems: These may result from unforeseen changes in national policy or government, or sudden unexpected political events. Insufficient government commitment may result. For example, in a project to encourage coastal communities to take-up aquaculture and discourage urban drift, there may be a change in government as opposed to financial incentives for farmers, and all subsidies and grants are cancelled. A project may also be disrupted by sudden internal strife.

Environmental problems: Environmental problems frequently arise and affect the project, or the project itself may cause environmental damage which is unacceptable. In the former case these may arise either from project-related or external natural factors unforeseen during project formulation, or from other projects which did not or were not planned at the time of project formulation. For example, in a project to enhance the fisheries of inland lakes and reservoirs through aquaculture, there may be sudden water pollution from new industrial projects nearby, or competition for the same water resources by urban development. There may also be general degradation of resources, or a natural disaster, such as an earthquake or a typhoon. In the second case, the production of shrimps in coastal ponds may produce a heavy discharge of nutrients from the complex causing algal blooms dangerous to traditional oyster fisheries nearby, or scouring may destroy more mangroves than initially foreseen and accepted.

Internal problems. Other problems may occur which may be related to the management and operation of the project itself. These may include the human factor where, for example, a difficult personality of one member of the management team causes minor conflict with other project staff or there may be a 'force-majeure'.

In summary, while it is the concern of the project formulation team to design the project to minimize all potential problems or risks in any of the above areas, soequally project management must anticipate them as far as possible and minimize their impact when they occur. It is apparent from this list of potential problem areas that many challengess which arise can be foreseen at the time of project design. Satisfactory project implementation, therefore, is dependent on sound project formulation.

CHAPTER EIGHT

Agribusiness Project Monitoring, Evaluation and Impact Assessment

8.1 Introduction

The process of monitoring, evaluation (M&E) and impact assessment is the primary means of collecting and analyzing information and is thus essential for good project management. In order to be used in a more positive manner, management and staff must have a common understanding of the importance of the process involved, and the contribution it can make to achieve the objectives of the technology development and transfer. For a project to be effective, monitoring, evaluation and impact assessment should be participatory

Whilst monitoring, and to a lesser extent ongoing evaluation, have been mentioned earlier, this chapter synthesizes the procedures to be used throughout the whole process from problem identification to diffusion of technology. The emphasis is on the process, not on individual project M & E.

8.2 Monitoring

Monitoring is a continuous assessment of both the functioning of the project activities in the context of implementation schedules and of the use of project inputs by the targeted population with regard to design expectations. The goals of monitoring are:

- To ensure that inputs, work schedules and outputs are proceeding according to plan, i.e., project implementation is on course;
- To provide record of input use, activities and results; and
- To detect E=early warning of deviations from initial goals and expected outcome.

Thus, monitoring is a process which systematically and critically observes events connected to a project in order to control the activities and adapt them to changing conditions. Key steps in the monitoring process are:

- Recording data on key indicators, largely available from existing sources, such as time sheets, and budget and supply records.
- Analysis performed at each functional level of management. This is important to assure the flow of both resources and technical information through the system.
- Reporting, often through quarterly and annual progress reports, oral presentations is organized by project staff.
- Storage, whether manual or computerized, should be accessible to managers at different levels of the system.

Monitoring is an internal project management tool. Integrating monitoring into implementation increases the accuracy of the collected information, reduces the cost of acquisition, increases the focus (alertness) of the participating planners and reduces the time lag for management corrections. Therefore, the emphasis is placed on simple methods. The various objectives of an M&E system are summarized in Box 8.1.

Box 8.1: Objectives of M & E

In the context of project, monitoring includes the periodic recording, analysis, reporting, and storage of data about key project and extension indicators. Data includes physical and financial information, details of inputs and services provided to beneficiaries, and data obtained from surveys and other recording mechanisms. Monitoring primarily provides information on project performance and gives signals on whether an activity is proceeding according to the plan. Monitoring is essential for evaluation.

8.3 Communication

It can also provide information on the socio-economic indicators for ex-post evaluation assessment. One could simultaneously monitor the resource use, i.e., of funds and personnel, as well as the process. Monitoring of the process may be accomplished through *inter alia* review meetings and periodic seminars. This permits management to compare the progress of work against planned activities, detect deviations, identify bottlenecks, and take corrective action while a project is in progress. Monitoring and evaluation are closely linked (see Figure 8.2).

8.4 Project Evaluation and its Typologies

Any assessment, appraisal, analysis or reviews are in a broad sense evaluative. Evaluations result in a set of recommendations which may address issues of planning, such as a shift in program objectives or contents or program implementation. Information from an evaluation is used in the management of technical programs, personnel, and financial resources. Evaluation in general addresses four important aspects of the program, namely: performance, quality, relevance and eventual impact.

- Performance compares achievements with expected output. It is primarily concerned with the use of resources and the timelines of the activity and is determined mostly through monitoring and on-going evaluation. However, assessing the success or failure of the project goes far beyond determining whether resources were used according to plan or activities were carried out on time.
- Quality deals with the adherence to accepted standards of scientific or technical work and precision. The quality of the project is determined almost exclusively through some form of peer expert review.
- Relevance of the project at each level investigates on the project relevance to objectives, which ultimately reflect developmental objectives. Relevance is closely related to the problem being addressed and the target group under consideration. Relevance is primarily assessed through peer or expert review.
- Impact deals with the effect of the project output on the ultimate users, often referred to as *"People level impact."*

8.4.1 Types of Evaluation

Evaluations are most often categorized according to when they occur in the project cycle and their purpose. Thus we have *ex-ante*, on-going, *ex-post* and impact evaluation.

- When it occurs before the event - to assess the potential impact of the project, it is called *ex-ante* project evaluation.

193

- When it occurs during the event - to evaluate the performance and quality of the project in progress, it is called on-going project evaluation.
- When it occur immediately after the event to determine the successful completion and relevance of the project, it is called *ex-post* project evaluation.
- When it occur several years after the project results have been achieved to assess its ultimate impact on development, it is called impact assessment.

8.4.1.1 Ex-ante Evaluation

Ex-ante evaluation is a project planning process which includes a comprehensive analysis of the potential impact of alternative activities before implementation. As the name implies, the evaluation is done prior to the initiation of the project. At this stage, not too much is known about the proposed project. Estimates of costs and benefits are sketchy, and the values assigned to them are only ballpark figures based on informal judgement.

Methods used are peer or expert reviews using checklists, scoring models, and even cost-benefit analysis. To make *ex-ante* evaluation more effective, there should be participation from different disciplines, and more comprehensive criteria must be applied. Through ex-ante evaluation, one could define the baseline against which progress will be measured, set targets, and state the assumptions used in making the projections. The indicators to be monitored should also be specified in order to give assistance to the ex-ante evaluation.

8.4.1.2 On-going Evaluation

On-going evaluations that are conducted throughout the project implementation are more useful for the project management than *ex-ante* and *ex-post* assessments. Here, on-going activities are reviewed at critical stages to determine if they should be continued, modified or aborted. They are used to analyze the use of resources, the quality of the project, and the continuing relevance of the projects. On-going evaluation is often conducted through peer reviews. They address problems associated with the day-to-day management of interventions and also can indicate the need for changes in project objectives and targets.

Monitoring is fundamental for on-going evaluation. It primarily tracks the provision and delivery of inputs and services, the generation of information on the ability and deployment of staff, infrastructure, equipment, supplies, services, and funds for projects within a program. In agribusiness projects, on-going evaluation is used to obtain feedback from the target group and is largely accomplished through a series of meetings at the site with peers, farmers, extension staff and NGOs.

8.4.1.3 Ex-post Evaluation (immediately after the completion)

An *ex-post* evaluation, or final evaluation, assess the project's performance, quality, and relevance immediately after the project completion. It attempts to measure the effectiveness and efficiency of a completed activity and includes an analysis of the original assumptions used in planning. A good *ex-post* evaluation is linked to *ex-ante* evaluation and can best be conducted where a baseline has been originally defined, targets have been projected, and data has been collected on important indicators. *Ex-post* evaluation is analyzed for the project from the beginning to the end, determining whether project objectives were attained, causes for discrepancies, costs, and the quality and relevance of the project. *Ex-post* evaluation often considers such aspects as the cost effectiveness of the project, its potential relevance to national development goals, the response of the project to an urgent and important problem, the acceptance of development agencies, and the results by farmers (end-users).

Common criteria for evaluating agribusiness projects are most notably quantity and quality of the anticipated project outcomes. These are not comprehensive enough to consider the appropriateness of the project outcomes or its value to development. Therefore, classical criteria need to be broadened to include end user satisfaction. The methods typically used for *ex-post* evaluation are statistical and economic evaluation, as well as agronomic and farmer/community assessment.

Advanced preparations for *ex-post* evaluation should include precise plans on documentation needed, people to interview and sites to visit. Some supplementary information may need to be gathered through surveys or interviews. Most evaluations use a blend of interviews, field visits, observations, and report writing. *Ex-post* evaluation also tries to clarify the internal and external factors affecting the outcome of the project.

Ex-post evaluation can provide important insights into the project process and provide a basis for comparing alternative organizational methodological approaches. The lessons learned could be systematically incorporated into subsequent evaluations making the processes much more relevant and efficient.

8.4.1.4 Impact Evaluation

This is a form of *ex-post* evaluation. Impact evaluation attempts to determine the extent to which projects have contributed to expected goals, such as increased farm production, or improved food security, etc. Typically, it is conducted several years after the results have been released making it less useful as a management tool than the other types of evaluation. *Ex-post* impact assessments are often used to convince policy makers to allocate more resources to projects.

If the project and program evaluations are to be used to support impact evaluations, this should be considered during *ex-ante* evaluations and the necessary baseline data and an M&E system should be set up in advance to serve this purpose.

Impact evaluation must distinguish between the contribution the project makes to national development from the contributions made by other factors such as existence of good extension services, agricultural inputs, adequate infrastructure, and favourable marketing and pricing policies. It has been shown that benefits are relatively easy to attribute in the case of single commodity technologies, such as high yielding varieties of rice under irrigation in Tabora for example. It has proved more difficult to do this in more diverse and complex systems as seen in most of sub-Saharan Africa.

The key concepts in *ex-post* impact assessments are causality, attribution, and incrementality.

Ex-post impact assessments usually require extensive and often expensive data collection and a thorough analysis of socio-economic factors. The results of impact evaluations have broad implications for future priority setting, not only for the project, but also for development support services. The types of impacts and methods used are discussed in the following sections.

8.5 Meaning of Impact

The term impact means different things to different people. In discussing the impact of any project, one can identify two broad categories of interpretations. In the first category, impact refers to the direct output of the activity, e.g., a variety, a breed, or a set of recommendations resulting from a project activity. Projects that generate products, often of biological nature, belong to this category. The second category goes beyond the direct product and tries to study its effects on the ultimate users, i.e. the so-called people level impact. The people level impact looks at how fit the project is within the overall R&D to discover facts (project) that have practical beneficial application (development) to society. Impact begins to occur only when there is a behavioural change among the potential users. This second type of impact deals with the actual adoption of the project output and subsequent effects on production, income, environment and/or whatever the development objectives may be.

The people level impact of any project activity cannot be assessed without information about the number of users(extent) and the degree or intensity of adoption of improved techniques, and the incremental effects of these techniques on production costs and output. The adoption of any technology is determined by several factors which are not part of the original project activity.

In any comprehensive impact assessment, there is, therefore, a need to differentiate between the project results and the contributions of the project to development, i.e., the people level impact, and both aspects should be addressed. Impact assessment is directed at establishing, with certainty, whether or not an intervention is producing its intended effect. A program that has a positive impact is one that achieves some positive movement or change in relation to objectives. This implies a set of operational defined goals and a criteria of success. There is also a need to establish that the outcome is the cause of some specified effort. As such, it is important to demonstrate that the changes observed are a function of the specific interventions and cannot be accounted for in any other way. As pointed out earlier the three basic principles to be observed in any impact study are causality, attribution, and incrementality.

8.6   Purpose of Impact Assessment

The purpose of undertaking an impact assessment prior to starting a project/program is to assist the project manager in planning and priority setting activities. This will enable one to study the likely economic impact of the proposed project activity and identify the optimal combination of research programs. By examining the relative benefits of different projects, it is possible to formulate priorities undertaken by the project. In addition, an *ex-ante* assessment can also provide a framework for gathering information to carry out an effective *ex-post* evaluation.

Given the resource constraints confronting project managers, *ex-ante* impact assessment is becoming a powerful planning tool in project management.   The various purposes for conducting an impact assessment after the completion of the project (*ex-post*) include:

- To study the impact and to provide feedback for managers, planners and policy makers;
- Lessons learned can be used to improve the management and decision making process with respect to priority setting, Implementation, and management of project activities as well as technology transfer,
- To improve accountability and transparency,
- To establish the credibility of the public sector, and; To justify increased budget allocations for project resources.

8.7   Overview of Impact Assessment Methods

A comprehensive impact assessment should simultaneously assess the various impacts of the agribusiness project. The various techniques and methods used to assess the different types of impact are summarized in Table 8.1 and discussed in the subsequent sections.

8.7.1   Direct Product of Project - Effectiveness Analysis

The most commonly used approach for assessing the direct product of the project is known as effectiveness analysis. A useful starting point for effectiveness analysis is the logical framework of the project (as discussed in chapter three). The logical framework permits the assessment of the degree to which the project activities have made changes in the desired direction. The logical framework itself is a simple matrix that provides a structure for one to specify the components of a program/ activity and the logical linkages between the set of means (inputs and activities) and the set of ends (outputs). This logical framework makes the impact assessment process transparent by explicitly stating the underlying assumptions of the analysis.

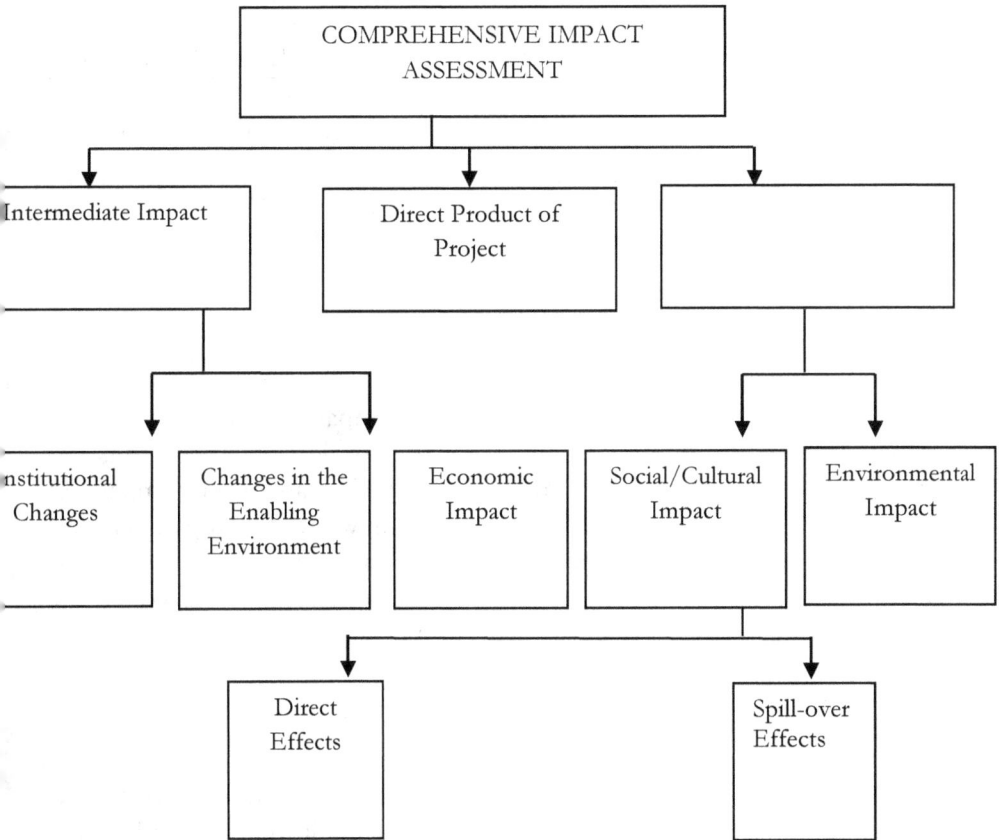

Figure 8.1: Comprehensive Impact Assessment
Source: Improved from Anandajayasekeram et al. (1996)

199

Table 8.1: **Impact Types, Techniques, and Methods Used in a Comprehensive Assessment**

IMPACT TYPE	TECHNIQUE	METHOD
INTERMEDIATE IMPACT • Institutional Changes • Changes in the Enabling Environment	Simple Comparison/Trend Analysis	Survey
DIRECT PRODUCT OF PROJECT	Simple Comparison - Target vs. Actual	Effectiveness Analysis Using Logical Framework
ECONOMIC IMPACT	Various	ROR Estimates
SOCIO-CULTURAL IMPACT	Comparison Over Time	Socio-economic Survey/ Adoption Survey
ENVIRONMENTAL IMPACT	Various • Qualitative • Quantitative • Need Bio-physical Information	Environmental Impact Assessment

The effectiveness analysis is a simple comparison of the targets to actual or observed performance of the project. Three sets of comparisons are identified in the literature: before and after comparison (also called historical comparison); with and without comparison; and target vs. achievement comparison. The most useful comparison is target vs. achieved. The targets need not be completely achieved for the project to be deemed effective. The movement in the direction of the desired target is enough evidence of project effectiveness.

8.8 Types of Impact

Indicators for impact studies are categorized into income, investment, social cultural, technology, participatory and environmental indicators. Examples for each of these categories are outlined below:

- **Income impact**
  - o Income change for company and community,
  - o Improved ability to provide for family,
  - o Increased income from sale,
  - o Better price for improved quality of the produce,
  - o Timing of sale to generate maximum returns,

- o Improved living standard - ownership of radio, bicycle, mobile phone,
- o Reduced production risk,
- o Number and type of jobs created,
- o Distribution of benefits
  — Gender
  — Income group
  — Location
- o Changes in resource allocation e.g. labour patterns
- o Nutritional Implications
- **Investment impact**
  - o Increase scale of farming – e.g. land areas in paprika production,
  - o Improved housing,
  - o Bought and built commercial plots,
  - o Improved soil fertility programmes,
  - o Better education for children,
  - o Improved ability to pay for school fees and other social amenities for the family,
- **Social / Cultural impact**
  - o Number of farming communities involved in paprika production,
  - o Changes in status of women,
  - o Changes in the knowledge and skill level of people,
  - o Changes in the health of various groups of people,
- **Indicators of participatory process impact**
  - o Joint field activities,
  - o Joint hosting of visitors and traders,
  - o Other informal joint activities,
  - o Other formal joint activities.
- **Knowledge of the technology impact**
  - o Improved methods of production among farming community,
  - o Increased ability of farming community to train others,
  - o Increased ability of the community to adapt the technology to own conditions.
- **Environmental impact**
  - o Reduced soil erosion and sedimentation,
  - o Reduced contamination of soil and water by herbicide or

pesticide residues,
- o Effects on the long-term functioning of biosphere, potential climate change, etc.,
- o Effects on biodiversity.
- **Institutional structures impact**
  - o Changes in intermediate organizational structures of methods and plans,
  - o Changes in the number and composition of scientists
  - o Changes in the proportion of funds budgeted to projects,
  - o Increase in proportion of equity to donor funds in project budget,
  - o Changes in the mix of public and private sector participation.

Bibliography

Abaza, H. (1992) (ed.). Appraisal methodology for sustainable development projects. UNEP Environment and Economics Unit. Record Id: MON-005828.

Anandajayasekeram, P. Martella, D.R and Rukuni, M. (1996). A Training Manual on R&D Evaluation and Impact Assessment of Investments in Agricultural and Natural Resources Research. Saccar, Gaborone.

Barlow, R. (1978). Land Resource Economics: The Economics of Real Estate. Prentice-Hall, Inc, Englewood Cliffs, New Jersey.

Baum, W.C and Tolbert, S.M. (1985). Investing in Development. Lessons of World Bank Experience. Finance and Development. The World Bank. Washington. DC.

Bergman, H and Boussard, J.M. (1976). Guide to the Economic Evaluation of Irrigation Projects. OECD. Paris.

DANIDA. (1996). Logical Framework Approach: A Flexible Tool for Participatory Development. Technical Advisory Service, DANIDA.

Dennis J. C. and Krishna, K. (1987). Project monitoring and evaluation in agriculture. IBRD, FAO, and IFAD. Record Id: MON-003444; ISBN 0-8018-3616-6.

DIF. (1991).Handbook of Cost-Benefit Analysis. Department of Finance. Canberra.

Douglas, F. B. and Jose, O. (1988). Sustainable resource management in agriculture and rural development projects : a review of bank policies, procedures and results. IBRD Environment Department. Record Id: MON-003467; Call No: Man-55 .

Eberhard G. and Germann, D. (1996.)The Concept of Participatory Impact Monitoring, GTZ; GmbH; Eschborn.

EU (1993). Manual of Project Cycle Management: Integrated Approach and Logical Framework. Commission of the European Communities Evaluation Unit Methods and Instruments for Project Cycle Management.

Gittinger, J.P. (1983). The Economic Analysis of Agricultural Projects. John Hopkins University Press, Baltimore, Maryland. ISBN 0-8018-2913-5.

Haynes, M. E. (1989) (rev ed.). Project management: from idea to implementation : a practical guide for success. Crisp Publications. Record Id: MON-009415.

HBS (1991). Project management Boston, MA, Harvard Business School Press. Record Id: MON-007247; ISBN 0-87584-264-X.

Horton D., P. Ballantyne, W. Peterson, Uribe, B., Grapasin, D. and Sheridan, K. (1993). Monitoring and Evaluating Agricultural Research: A Source Book. ISNAR, The Hague, The Netherlands.

Imboden, N. (1978). A Management Approach to Project Appraisal and Evaluation. Development Centre Studies, OECD.

Irwin, G. (1978). Modern Cost-Benefit Methods: An Introduction to Financial, Economic and Social Appraisal of Development Projects. MacMillan Education, London.

Little, I.M.D, and Mirrlees, J.A. (1980). Project Appraisal and Planning for Developing Countries. London: Heinemann.

Macmillan, J., Mudimu, G., Rugube, L. and Guveya, E. (1992). Measuring benefits and costs of wheat projects: Zambia and Tanzania. Department of Agricultural Economics and Farm Management, the University of Manitoba, Winnipeg, Manitoba.

Markandya, A. Pearce, D. (1988). Environmental considerations and the choice of the discount rate in developing countries. IBRD Environment Department. Record Id: MON-003468.

McLean D. (1988). Monitoring and Evaluation in the Management of Agricultural Research. Working Paper No.14, ISNAR, The Hague.

McLean, D (1990). The Logical Framework in Research Planning and E valuation. Working Paper No 12, ISNAR, The Hague, The Netherlands

Norman, L. and Wood, C. (1980). Methods of environmental impact assessment for use in project appraisal and physical planning. Univerity of Manchester.

OECD (1994). Project and policy appraisal: Integrating economics and environment Record Id: MON-007314; ISBN 92-64-14107-3.

OECD. (1986). The public management of forestry projects. Record Id: MON-001428; ISBN 92-64-12826-3.

OECD. (1989). The impact of development projects on poverty. Development Centre, Inter-American Development Bank. Record Id: MON-003439; ISBN 92-64-13162-0.

OIC (1983). Project evaluation management. Record Id: MON-000745; ISBN 92-9047-103-7; Call No: X-Man-PRO-14.

Olof, M (1981). An institutional approach to project analysis in developing countries. OECD. Development Centre Record Id: MON-005158; ISBN 92-64-12226-5

Overseas Development Administration (1995). A guide to social analysis for projects in developing countries. Record Id: MON-008574; ISBN 0-11-580258-4.

Robert, S. and Alan, W. (1988). The principles of practical cost-benefit analysis. Oxford Univeity Press. Oxford. Record Id: MON-002870; ISBN 0-19-877041-3.

Squire, J. and Van Der Tak, H.G. (1975). Economic Analysis of Projects. John Hopkins University Press, World Bank, New York.

Tisdell, C. (1985). Project Evaluation and Social-Cost Benefit Analysis In LDCs: Awkward Issues for a Useful Approach. *Development Southern Africa*, 2(1).

Van Rooyen, C.J. (1986). Guidelines for Economic Analysis of Agricultural Development Projects. *Development Southern Africa*, 3(4).

Ward, A W, Deren, B.J, and D'Silva, E H, (1991). The Economics of Project Analysis, A Practitioner's Guide. Economic Development Institute of the World Bank, The World Bank Washington, DC, USA.

World Bank, 1979. Costs and Benefits of Agricultural Research: The State of the Art. World Bank Staff Working Paper No 360, Washington, DC.

Appendix 1: Rates and Factor Tables

Table A.1: Future Value Interest Factors

1%	2%	3%	4%	5%	6%	7%	8%	9%	10%	11%	12%	13%
1.000	1.000	1.000	1.000	1.000	1.000	1.000	1.000	1.000	1.000	1.000	1.000	1.000
1.010	1.020	1.030	1.040	1.050	1.060	1.070	1.080	1.090	1.100	1.110	1.120	1.130
1.020	1.040	1.061	1.082	1.102	1.124	1.145	1.166	1.188	1.210	1.232	1.254	1.277
1.030	1.061	1.093	1.125	1.158	1.191	1.225	1.260	1.295	1.331	1.368	1.405	1.443
1.041	1.082	1.126	1.170	1.216	1.262	1.311	1.360	1.412	1.464	1.518	1.574	1.630
1.051	1.104	1.159	1.217	1.276	1.338	1.403	1.469	1.539	1.611	1.685	1.762	1.842
1.052	1.126	1.194	1.265	1.340	1.419	1.501	1.587	1.677	1.772	1.870	1.974	2.082
1.072	1.149	1.230	1.316	1.407	1.504	1.606	1.714	1.828	1.949	2.076	2.211	2.353
1.083	1.172	1.267	1.369	1.477	1.594	1.718	1.851	1.993	2.144	2.305	2.476	2.658
1.094	1.195	1.305	1.423	1.551	1.689	1.838	1.999	2.172	2.358	2.558	2.773	3.004
1.105	1.219	1.344	1.480	1.629	1.791	1.967	2.159	2.367	2.594	2.839	3.106	3.395
1.116	1.243	1.384	1.539	1.710	1.898	2.105	2.332	2.580	2.853	3.152	3.479	3.836
1.127	1.268	1.426	1.601	1.796	2.012	2.252	2.518	2.813	3.138	3.498	3.896	4.335
1.138	1.294	1.469	1.665	1.886	2.133	2.410	2.720	3.056	3.452	3.883	4.363	4.898
1.149	1.319	1.513	1.732	1.930	2.261	2.579	2.937	3.342	3.797	4.310	4.887	5.535
1.161	1.346	1.558	1.801	2.079	2.397	2.759	3.172	3.642	4.177	4.785	5.474	6.254
1.173	1.373	1.605	1.873	2.183	2.540	2.952	3.426	3.970	4.595	5.311	6.130	7.067
1.184	1.400	1.653	1.948	2.292	2.693	3.159	3.700	4.328	5.054	5.895	6.866	7.986
1.196	1.428	1.702	2.026	2.407	2.854	3.380	3.996	4.717	5.560	6.544	7.690	9.024
1.208	1.457	1.754	2.107	2.527	3.026	3.617	4.316	5.142	6.116	7.263	8.613	10.197
1.220	1.486	1.806	2.191	2.653	3.207	3.870	4.661	5.604	6.728	8.062	9.646	11.523
1.282	1.641	2.094	2.666	3.386	4.292	5.427	6.848	8.623	10.835	13.585	17.00	21.231
1.348	1.811	2.417	3.243	4.322	5.743	7.612	10.0634	13.268	17.449	22.892	29.960	39.116

Table A.1 Continued

Period n	14%	15%	16%	17%	18%	19%	20%	24%	28%	32%	36%	40%
0	1.000	1.000	1.000	1.000	1.000	1.000	1.000	1.000	1.000	1.000	1.000	1.000
1	1.140	1.150	1.160	1.170	1.180	1.190	1.200	1.240	1.280	1.320	1.360	1.400
2	1.300	1.322	1.346	1.369	1.392	1.416	1.440	1.538	1.638	1.742	1.850	1.960
3	1.482	1.521	1.562	1.602	1.643	1.685	1.728	1.907	2.097	2.300	2.515	2.744
4	1.689	1.749	1.811	1.874	1.939	2.005	2.074	2.364	2.684	3.036	3.421	3.842
5	1.925	2.011	2.100	2.192	2.288	2.386	2.488	2.392	3.436	4.007	4.653	5.378
6	2.195	2.313	2.436	2.565	2.700	2.840	2.986	3.635	4.398	5.290	6.328	7.530
7	2.502	2.660	2.826	3.001	3.185	3.379	3.583	4.508	5.629	6.983	8.605	10.541
8	2.853	3.059	3.278	5.11	3.759	4.021	4.300	5.590	7.206	9.217	11.703	14.758
9	3.252	3.518	3.803	4.108	4.435	4.785	5.160	6.931	9.223	12.166	15.917	20.661
10	3.707	4.046	4.411	4.807	5.234	5.695	6.192	8.549	11.806	16.060	21.647	28.925
11	4.226	4.652	5.117	5.624	6.176	6.777	7.430	10.657	15.112	21.199	29.439	40.494
12	4.818	5.350	5.936	6.580	7.288	8.064	8.916	13.215	19.343	27.983	40.037	56.694
13	5.492	6.153	6.886	7.699	8.599	9.596	10.699	16.386	24.759	36.937	54.451	76.372
14	6.261	7.076	7.988	9.007	10.147	11.420	12.839	20.319	31.961	48.757	74.053	111.12
15	7.138	8.137	9.226	10.539	11.974	13.590	15.407	25.196	40.565	64.359	100.712	155.56
16	8.137	9.358	10.748	12.330	14.129	16.172	18.488	31.243	51.923	84.954	136.969	217.79
17	9.276	10.761	12.468	14.426	16.672	19.244	22.186	38.741	66.461	112.139	186.278	304.91
18	10.575	12.375	14.463	16.879	19.673	22.901	26.623	48.039	85.071	148.023	253.338	426.87
19	12.056	14.232	16.777	19.748	23.214	27.252	31.948	59.568	108.890	195.391	344.540	597.63
20	13.743	16.367	19.461	23.106	27.393	32.429	38.338	73.864	139.380	257.916	468.574	836.68
25	26.462	32.919	40.874	50.658	62.669	77.388	95.396	216.542	478.905	1033.590	2180.081	4499.8
30	50.950	66.212	85.850	111.065	143.371	184.675	237.376	634.820	164.504	414.075	10143.019	24201

Table A.2: Future Value Interest Factor for an Annuity

riod	1%	2%	3%	4%	5%	6%	7%	8%	9%	10%	11%	12%	13%
	1.000	1.000	1.000	1.000	1.000	1.000	1.000	1.000	1.000	1.000	1.000	1.000	1.000
	2.010	2.020	2.030	2.040	2.050	2.060	2.070	2.080	2.090	2.100	2.110	2.120	2.130
	3.030	3.060	3.091	3.122	3.152	3.184	3.215	3.246	3.278	3.310	3.342	3.342	3.407
	4.060	4.122	4.184	4.246	4.310	4.375	4.440	4.506	4.573	4.641	4.710	4.779	4.850
	5.101	5.204	5.309	5.416	5.526	5.637	5.751	5.867	5.985	6.105	6.228	6.353	6.480
	6.152	6.308	6.468	6.633	6.802	6.975	7.153	7.336	7.523	7.716	7.913	8.115	8.323
	7.214	7.434	7.662	7.898	8.142	8.394	8.654	8.923	9.200	9.487	9.783	10.089	10.405
	8.286	8.583	8.892	9.214	9.549	9.897	10.260	10.637	11.028	11.346	11.859	12.300	12.757
	9.369	9.755	10.159	10.583	11.027	11.491	11.978	12.488	13.021	13.579	14.164	14.776	15.416
	10.462	10.950	11.464	12.006	12.578	13.181	13.816	14.487	15.193	15.937	16.722	17.549	18.420
	11.567	12.169	12.808	13.486	14.207	14.972	15.784	16.645	17.560	18.531	19.561	20.655	21.814
	12.683	13.412	14.192	15.026	15.917	16.870	17.888	18.977	20.141	21.384	22.713	24.133	25.650
	13.809	14.680	15.618	16.627	17.713	18.882	20.141	21.495	22.953	24.523	26.212	28.029	29.985
	14.947	15.974	17.086	18.292	19.599	21.015	22.550	24.215	26.019	27975	30.095	32.393	34.883
	16.097	17.293	18.599	20.024	21.579	23.276	25.129	27/152	29.361	31.772	34.405	37.280	40.417
	17.258	18.639	20.1578	21.825	23.657	25.673	27.888	30.324	33.003	35.950	39.190	42.753	46.672
	18.430	20.012	21.762	23.698	25.840	28.213	30.840	33.750	36.974	40.545	44.501	48.884	55.739
	19.615	21.412	23.414	25.645	28.132	30.906	33.999	37.450	41.301	45.599	50.396	55.750	61.725
	20.811	22.841	25.117	27.671	30.539	33.760	37.379	41.446	46.018	51.259	56.939	63.440	70.749
	22.019	24.297	26.870	29.778	33.066	36.786	40.995	45.762	51.160	57.275	64.203	72.052	80.947
	28.243	32.030	36.459	41.646	47.727	54.865	63.249	73.106	84.701	98.347	114.413	133.334	155.620
	34.785	40.568	47.575	56.805	66.459	79.058	94.461	113.283	136.308	164.494	199.021	241.333	293.199

Table A.2 Continued

Period n	14%	15%	16%	17%	18%	19%	20%	24%	28%	32%	36%	40%
1	1.000	1.000	1.000	1.000	1.000	1.000	1.000	1.000	1.000	1.000	1.000	1.000
2	2.140	2.150	2.160	2.170	2.180	2.190	2.200	2.240	2.280	2.320	2.360	2.400
3	3.440	3.473	3.506	3.539	3.572	3.606	3.640	3.778	3.918	4.062	4.210	4.360
4	4.921	4.993	5.066	5.141	5.215	5.291	5.368	5.6845	6.016	6.362	6.725	7.104
5	6.610	6.742	6.877	7.014	7.154	7.297	7.442	8.048	8.700	9.398	10.146	10.946
6	8.536	8.754	8.977	9.207	9.442	9.683	9.930	10.980	12.136	13.406	14.799	16.324
7	10.730	11.067	11.414	11.772	12.142	12.523	12.916	14.615	16.534	18.696	21.126	23.853
8	13.233	13.727	14.240	14.773	15.327	15.902	16.499	19.123	22.163	25.678	29.732	34.395
9	16.085	16.786	17.518	18.285	19.086	19.923	20.799	24.7123	29.369	34.895	41.435	49.153
10	19.337	20.304	21.321	22.393	23.521	24.709	25.959	31.643	38.592	47.062	57.352	69.814
11	23.044	24.349	25.733	27.200	28.755	30.404	32.150	40.238	50.399	63.122	78.998	98.739
12	27.271	29.002	30.850	32.824	34.931	37.180	39.580	50.985	65.510	84.320	108.437	139.23
13	32.089	34.352	36.786	39.404	42.219	45.244	48.497	64.110	84.854	112.303	148.475	195.92
14	37.581	40.505	43.672	47.103	50.818	54.841	59.196	80.496	109.612	149.240	202.926	275.30
15	43.842	47.580	51.660	56.110	60.965	66.261	72.035	100.815	141.303	197.997	276.979	386.42
16	50.980	55.717	60.925	66.649	72.939	79.850	87.442	126.011	181.868	262.356	377.692	541.98
17	59.118	65.075	71.673	78.979	87.068	96.022	105.931	157.253	233.791	347.310	514.661	759.78
18	68.394	75.836	84.141	93.406	103.740	115.266	128.117	195.994	300.252	459.449	700,939	1064.6
19	78.969	88.212	98.603	110.285	123.414	138.166	154.740	244.033	385.323	607.474	954.277	1491.5
20	91.025	102.44	115.380	130.033	146.628	165.418	186.688	303.601	494.213	802.863	1298.817	2089.2
25	181.871	212.793	249.214	292.105	342.603	402.042	471.981	898.098	1706.803	3226.844	6053.004	11247.
30	356.787	434.745	530.321	647.439	790.948	966.712	1181.882	2604.916	5873.231	12940.859	28172.276	60501.

Table A.3: Present Value Interest Factor

iod	1%	2%	3%	4%	5%	6%	7%	8%	0%	10%	11%	12%	13%
	1.000	1.000	1.000	1.000	1.000	1.000	1.000	1.000	1.000	1.000	1.000	1.000	1.000
	0.990	0.980	0.971	0.962	0.952	0.943	0.935	0.926	0.917	0.909	0.901	0.893	0.885
	0.980	0.961	0.943	0.925	0.907	0.890	0.873	0.857	0.842	0.826	0.812	0.797	0.783
	0.971	0.942	0.915	0.889	0.864	0.840	0.816	0.794	0.772	0.751	0.731	0.712	0.693
	0.961	0.924	0.889	0.8655	0.823	0.792	0.765	0.735	0.708	0.683	0.659	0.636	0.613
	0.951	0.906	0.863	0.822	0.784	0.747	0.715	0.681	0.650	6.621	0.593	0.567	0.543
	0.942	0.888	0.838	0.790	0.746	0.705	0.666	0.630	0.596	0.564	0.535	0.507	0.480
	0.933	0.871	0.813	0.760	0.711	0.665	0.623	0.585	0.547	0.513	0.482	0.452	0.425
	0.923	0.853	0.789	0.731	0.677	0.627	0.582	0.540	0.502	0.467	0.434	0/404	0.376
	0.914	0.837	0.766	0.703	0.645	0.592	0.544	0.500	0.460	0.424	0.391	0.361	0.333
	0.905	0.820	0.744	0.676	0.614	0.554	0.508	0.463	0.422	0.386	0.352	0.322	0.295
	0.96	0.804	0.722	0.650	0.585	0.527	0.4475	0.4219	0.388	0.350	0.317	0.287	0.261
	0.887	0.788	0.701	0.625	0.557	0.497	0.444	0.397	0.356	0.319	0.286	0.257	0.251
	0.879	0.773	0.681	0.601	0.550	0.469	0.415	0.368	0.326	0.290	0.258	0.229	0.204
	0.870	0.758	0.661	0.577	0.505	0.442	0.388	0.340	0.229	0.263	0.232	0.205	0.181
	0.861	0.743	0.642	0.555	0.481	0.417	0.363	0.315	0.275	0.239	0.209	0.183	0.160
	0.853	0.728	0.623	0.534	0.458	0.394	0.339	0.292	0.252	0.218	0.188	0.163	0.141
	0.844	0.714	0.605	0.513	0.436	0.371	0.317	0.270	0.231	0.198	0.170	0.146	0.125
	0.836	0.700	0.587	0.494	0.416	0.350	0.296	0.250	0.212	0.180	0.153	0.130	0.111
	0.828	0.686	0.570	0.475	0.396	0.331	0.276	0.232	0.194	0.164	0.138	0.116	0.098
	0.820	0.673	0.554	0.456	0.337	0.512	0.258	0.215	0.178	0.149	0.214	0.104	0.087
	0.780	0.610	0.478	0.375	0.295	0.233	0.184	0.146	0.116	0.092	0.074	0.059	0.047
	0.742	00.552	0.412	0.308	0.251	0.174	0.131	0.099	0.075	0.057	0.0 44	0.053	0.026

Table A.3 continued

Period n	14%	15%	16%	17%	18%	19%	20%	24%	28%	32%	36%	40%
0	1.000	1.000	1.000	1.000	1.000	1.000	1.000	1.000	1.000	1.000	1.000	1.000
1	0.877	0.870	0.862	0.855	0.847	0.840	0.833	0.806	0.781	0.758	0.735	0.714
3	0.769	0.756	0.743	0.731	0.718	0.706	0.694	0.650	0.610	0.574	0.541	0.510
4	0.675	0.572	0.552	0.534	0.516	0.499	0.482	0.423	0.373	0.329	0.292	0.260
5	0.519	0.497	0.476	0.456	0.437	0.419	0.402	0.341	0.291	0.250	0.215	0.186
6	0.456	0.432	0.410	0.390	0.370	0.352	0.335	0.275	0.227	0.189	0.158	0.133
7	0.400	0.376	0.354	0.333	0.314	0.296	0.297	0.222	0.718	0.143	0.116	0.095
8	0.351	0.327	0.305	0.285	0.266	0.249	0.233	0.179	0.139	0.108	0.085	0.068
9	0.308	0.284	0.264	0.243	0.226	0.209	0.194	0.144	0.108	0.082	0.063	0.048
10	0.270	0.247	0.227	0.208	0.191	0.176	0.162	0.116	0.085	0.062	0.046	0.035
11	0.237	0.215	00.195	0.178	0.162	0.148	0.135	0.094	0.066	0.040	0.034	0.025
12	0.208	0.187	0.168	0.152	0.137	0.124	0.112	0.076	0.052	0.036	0.025	0.018
13	0.182	0.163	0.145	0.130	0.116	0.104	0.093	0.061	0.040	0.027	0018	0.013
14	0.160	0.141	0.125	0.111	0.099	o.088	0.078	0.049	0.032	0.021	0.014	0.009
15	0.140	0.123	0.108	0.095	0.084	0.074	0.065	0.040	0.025	0.016	0.010	0.006
16	0.123	0.107	0.093	0.081	0.071	0.062	0.054	0.032	0.019	0.012	0.007	0.005
17	0.108	0.093	0.080	0.069	0.060	0.052	0.045	0.026	0.015	0.009	0.005	0.003
18	0.095	0.081	0.069	0.059	0.051	0.044	0.038	0.021	0.012	0.007	0.004	0.002
19	0.083	0.070	0.060	0.051	0.045	0.037	0.051	0.017	0.009	0.005	0.004	0.002
20	0.073	0.061	0.051	0.043	0.057	0.051	0.026	0.014	0.007	0.004	0.002	0.001
25	0.038	0.030	0.024	0.020	0.016	0.013	0.010	0.005	0.002	0.001	0.000	0.000
30	0.020	0.015	0.012	0.009	0.007	0.005	0.004	0.002	0.001	0.000	0.000	0.000

Table A.4: Present Value Interest Factor for an Annuity

riod	1%	2%	3%	4%	5%	6%	7%	8%	0%	10%	11%	12%	13%
	1.000	1.000	1.000	1.000	1.000	1.000	1.000	1.000	1.000	1.000	1.000	1.000	1.000
	0.990	0.980	0.971	0.962	0.952	0.943	0.935	0.926	0.917	0.909	0.901	0.893	0.885
	1.970	1.942	1.913	1.886	1.859	1.833	1.808	1.783	1.759	1.736	1.713	1.690	1.668
	2.941	2.884	2.829	2.775	2.723	2.673	2.624	2.577	2.531	2.487	2.444	2.402	2.361
	3.902	3.808	3.717	3.630	3.546	3.465	3.387	3.312	3.240	3.170	3.102	3.037	2.974
	4.853	4.713	4.580	4.452	4.329	4.212	4.100	3.993	3.890	3.791	3.696	3.605	3.517
	5.595	5.601	5.417	5.242	5.076	4.917	4.766	4.623	4.486	4.355	4.232	4.111	3.998
	6.728	6.472	6/230	6/002	5.786	5.582	5.389	5.206	5.033	4.868	4.712	4.564	4.423
	7.652	7.325	7.020	6.733	6.463	6.210	5.971	5.747	5.535	6.335	5.146	4.968	1.799
	8.566	8.162	7.786	7.435	7.08	6.802	6.515	6.247	5.995	5.759	5.537	5.328	5.132
	9.741	8.983	8.530	8.111	7.722	7.360	7.024	6.710	6.418	6.145	5.889	5.650	5.426
	10.368	9.787	9.253	8.760	8.306	7.887	7.499	7.139	6.805	6.495	6.207	5.938	5.687
	11.255	10.575	9.954	9.385	8.863	8.384	7.945	7.536	7.161	6.814	6.492	6.194	5.918
	12.134	11.348	10.635	9.986	9.394	8.853	8.358	7.904	7.487	7.103	6.750	6.424	6.122
	13.004	12.106	11.296	10.563	9.899	9.295	8.745	8.244	7.786	7.367	6.982	6.628	6.302
	13.865	12.849	11.938	11.118	10.380	9.712	9.108	8.559	8.060	7.606	7.191	6.811	6.462
	14.718	13.578	12.561	11.652	10.838	10.106	9.447	8.851	8.312	7.824	7.379	6.974	6.604
	15.562	14.292	13.166	12.166	11.274	10.477	9.763	9.122	8.544	8.022	7.549	7.120	6.729
	16.398	14.992	13.754	12.659	11.960	10.828	10.059	9.372	8.756	8.201	7.702	7.250	6.840
	17.226	14.992	13.754	12.659	11.690	10.828	10.059	9.372	8.756	8.201	7.702	7.250	6.840
	18.046	16.351	14.877	13.590	12.462	11.470	10.594	9.818	9.128	8.514	7.963	7.469	7.025
	22.023	19.523	17.413	15.622	14.094	12.783	11.654	10.675	9.823	9.077	8.422	7.843	7.330
	25.808	22.397	19.600	17.292	15.373	13.765	12.409	11.258	10.274	9.427	8.694	8.055	7.496

Table A.4 continued

Period n	14%	15%	16%	17%	18%	19%	20%	24%	28%	32%	36%	40%
0	1.000	1.000	1.000	1.000	1.000	1.000	1.000	1.000	1.000	1.000	1.000	1.000
1	0.877	0.870	0.862	0.855	0.847	0.840	0.833	0.806	0.781	0.758	0.735	0.714
2	1.647	1.626	1.605	1.585	1.566	1.547	1.528	1.457	1.392	1.332	1.276	1.224
3	2.322	2.283	2.246	2.210	2.174	2.140	2.106	1.981	1.868	1.766	1.674	1.589
4	2.914	2.855	2.798	2.743	2.690	2.639	2.589	2.404	2.241	2.096	1.966	1.849
5	3.433	3.352	3.274	3.199	3.127	3.058	2.991	2.745	2.532	2.345	2.181	2.035
6	3.889	3.784	3.685	3.589	3.498	3.410	3.326	3.020	2.759	2.534	2.339	2.168
7	4.288	4.160	4.039	3.922	3.812	3.706	3.605	3.242	2.937	2.678	2.455	2.263
8	4.639	4.487	4.344	4.207	4.078	3.954	3.837	3.421	3.076	2.786	2.540	2.331
9	4.946	4.772	4.607	4.451	4.303	4.163	4.031	3.566	3.184	2.868	2.603	2.379
10	5.216	5.019	4.883	4.659	4.494	4.339	4.193	3.682	3.269	2.930	2.650	2.414
11	5.453	4.234	5.029	4.836	4.656	4.486	4.327	3.776	3.335	2.978	2.683	2.438
12	5.660	5.421	5.197	4.988	4.793	4.611	4.439	3.851	3.387	3.013	2.708	2.456
13	5.842	5.583	5.342	5.118	4.910	4.715	4.533	3.912	3.427	3.040	2.727	2.469
14	6.002	5.724	5.468	5.229	5.008	4.802	4.611	3.962	3.459	3.061	2.740	2.478
15	6.142	5.847	5.575	5.324	5.092	4.876	4.675	4.001	3.483	3.076	2.750	2.484
16	6.265	5.954	5.669	5.405	5.162	4.938	4.730	4.033	3.503	3.088	2.758	2.489
17	6.373	6.047	5.749	5.475	5.222	4.990	4.775	4.059	3.518	3.097	2.763	2.492
18	6.647	6.128	5.818	5.534	5.273	5.033	4.812	4.080	3.529	3.104	2.763	2.492
19	6.550	6.198	5.877	5.584	5.316	5.070	4.844	4.097	3.539	3.109	2.770	2.496
20	6.623	6.259	5.929	6.628	5.353	5.101	4.870	1.110	3.516	3.113	2.772	2.497
25	6.873	6.464	6.097	5.766	5.467	5.195	4.948	4.147	3.564	3.122	2.776	2.499
30	7.003	6.566	6.177	5.829	5.517	5.235	4.979	4.160	3.569	3.124	2.778	2.500

Book Overview

In the context of a developing country like Tanzania, almost all employees in both the private and public domains are increasingly involved in designing, analysis, management and evaluation of projects. Most of them find themselves carrying out project related activities often in complex, messy, and poorly controlled situations. For example, practitioners and professionals (e.g. in agriculture, education, health, industry) are often required to become involved in project management, and appraisal but find it difficult due to lack of hands on skills.

Agribusiness Project Appraisal is the first context specific book of its kind to provide a complete methodology for managing projects in agriculture. It gives advice and support in the carrying out of project planning execution and evaluation. The emphasis of this book is on achieving a thorough and rigorous social and economic analysis through systematic procedures appropriate to project management. Particular features include:

- Key concepts of project planning.
- The log-frame approach to project management
- Cost Benefit Analysis of the project
- Techniques of project analysis
- Implementation of the project and
- Project monitoring, evaluation and impact assessment

Whether new or experienced in project management, readers will find this book an invaluable resource for initiating, planning, executing, and closing projects as it skilfully guide them through the critical phases of the project life cycle. Though relevant to management of all types of projects, the perspective of this book is that of Agribusiness.

About the Authors

Joseph P. Hella (PhD), is an Associate Professor of Agricultural Economics in the Department of Food and Resource Economics and the former Associate Director of Postgraduate Studies at the Sokoine University of Agriculture (SUA). He teaches Project Appraisal and Farm Management to both undergraduate and graduate students. He writes extensively on the agricultural economics of arid and semi-arid climates and climate adaptation in Africa.

Daniel W. Ndyetabula (PhD), is a Lecturer of Business Economics in the Department of Agricultural Economics and Agribusiness and the coordinator of Postgraduate Studies at the School of Agricultural Economics and Business Studies (SAEBS) of SUA. He teaches Agribusiness Finance, and Project Appraisal. His current research interests lies on the interplay between agribusiness value chain financing, penetration of processed food into dietary patterns of consumers and innovation, including the role innovation can play in creating a vibrant private sector.

Index

J

Jargon, 169

K

Kikwete, Jakaya, 18
Kilimo Kwanza, 18

L

Log-frame Matrix, 58
Logical Framework Approach, 47, 203

M

Market interest rates, 103, 112
Ministry of Agriculture and Food Security, 184
Miombo Fisheries Project, 184

N

National Agriculture and Food Corporation, 24
National integration, 111
Ndyetabula, Daniel W, 216
Need based projects, 29
Net Present Value, xv, 36, 112, 128, 129, 132, 133, 134, 135, 137, 141, 147, 148
Network analysis, 157, 163, 166, 169, 171
Network-On-Arrow, 167

O

Objectives analysis, 52
Operating costs, 148
Opportunity cost, 104, 114, 127
Organization Breakdown Structure, 162
Over-regulation, 17

P

Pareto Principle, 106
Participation analysis, 37
Pay Back Period, xv, 129, 131, 132
Payback period, 131, 144
Perpetuity, 126
Physical goods, 67
Physical production inputs, 111
Polaris Submarine project, 167
Political risk assessment, 42
Precedence Diagram Method, 167
Problem Areas in Project Implementation, 187
Program Evaluation and Review Technique, 164
Project streams, 145

R

Repayment Capacity, 91, 92
Reporting interfaces, 162
Resource based projects, 29
Response time, 161
Responsibility, 162
Retained earnings, 127
Return on Investment, 132
Risk, 28, 91, 114, 115, 143
Risk adjusted discount rate, 146

S

Safety Margins, 147
Scheduling, 155, 156, 159, 163, 181, 188
Self-liquidating loans, 91
Senkondo, M.M., xiii
Sensitivity analysis, xv, 106, 108, 113, 143, 144, 147, 152
Shadow prices, 74, 112
Social Accounting Matrix model, 109
Social analysis, 102

Sokoine University of Agriculture, 216
Statutory regulations, 156
Surrogate prices, 74
Switching Values, 147

T

Tanzania National Business Council, 18
Tradable and non-tradable goods, 80
Traore, Karim, ii
Tree Project Network, 172

U

Ujamaa, 17

V

Variable Repayment Plan, 96

W

Work Breakdown Structure, 162
World Bank, 20, 203, 205
World prices, 74

www.ingramcontent.com/pod-product-compliance
Lightning Source LLC
Chambersburg PA
CBHW070418270326
41926CB00014B/2835